St. Paul's Anglican Church, Falmouth

Also by Michael Nathan-Pepple:
Travel Guide: *All About Antigua and Barbuda*
ebook available on Amazon: https://www.amazon.co.uk/All-About-Antigua-Barbuda-attractionsebook/dp/B0BP9TQSSQ

©2023 Michael Nathan-Pepple
Published by Michael Nathan-Pepple
mnathanpepple@gmail.com

The rights of the author to be identified as the Author of this Work have been asserted in accordance with the Copyright, Designs and Patents Act 1988.

All rights reserved. No part of this publication may be reproduced, stored in a retrieval system or transmitted, in any form or by any means, electronic, mechanical, photocopying or otherwise, without the prior permission of the publisher.

ISBN:978-1-9162807-1-7

Photographs by Michael Nathan-Pepple

Layout and Printing by www.beamreachuk.co.uk

Historical Churches
OF THE CARIBBEAN ISLAND OF

Antigua

An overview of the complex relationship between the older established churches, slavery and their black converts.

Written by

Michael Nathan-Pepple

Contents

Acknowledgements 6

Introduction 7

1 Historical Context 9
Arrival and ill-treatment of enslaved Africans 10
Christianity in Africa before the trans-Atlantic slave trade 11
African spiritual practices 13

2 Background of the four main Christian denominations 15
Anglican 15
Moravian 18
Methodist 20
Roman Catholic 23

3 The connection between European Christianity and the Trans-Atlantic Slave Trade 25
Christian Churches and the trans-Atlantic slave trade 25
Evangelical Revival and the abolition of slavery 27
Conversion of enslaved Africans to Christianity 27
Apology and reparation for the slave trade 28

Conclusion 30

4 Historical Churches of Antigua 33

Anglican 34
St Paul's Anglican Church 34
St. Barnabas Anglican Church 35
St. George's Anglican Church 36
Our Lady Of The Valley Anglican Church 37

St. Philip's Anglican Church 38
St. Peter's Anglican Church 39
St. John's Cathedral Anglican Church 40
All Saints Anglican Church 41

Moravian 43
Spring Gardens Moravian Church 43
Gracehill Moravian Church 44
Cedar Hall Moravian Church 45
Lebanon Moravian Church 46
Greenbay Moravian Church 47
Gracefield Moravian Church 48
Gracebay Moravian Church 49
Cana Moravian Church 50

Methodist 52
Ebenezer Methodist Church 52
Parham Methodist Church 53
Gilbert Memorial Methodist Church 54
Bethesda Methodist Church 55
Baxter Memorial Methodist Church 56
Freemansville Methodist Church 57

Roman Catholic 59
St Joseph's and St Patrick's Catholic Church 59
Our Lady of Perpetual Help Church 60

Conclusion 62

References: *63*

Acknowledgements

I would like to start by thanking my awesome wife, Sheralyn Nathan-Pepple, who firmly stood by my side when I commenced research for this book. She read the early and later drafts and gave advice on the contents and structure of the book. In addition, she navigated as I drove around Antigua to capture the magnificent pictures of the historical churches. Therefore, it is not an exaggeration to say that she played an important role in getting this book completed. Also, my profound gratitude and thanks goes to Julie Campbell, who made the time to proof read the book. I sincerely thank her for her honesty, methodical approach and useful suggestions.

Furthermore, I give thanks to the Creator and my ancestors for giving me the inspiration to write such an interesting and thought-provoking book, which gives a glimpse into the past and how enslaved Africans were able to overcome and survive the brutality of slavery. It is anticipated that their descendants in Antigua and Barbuda, the Caribbean region and all across the Americas will never forget their struggle and pain.

Special thanks are due to Reverend Derek Browne of the Methodist Church, Desmond Thomas of Gracefield Moravian Church and Serene Christopher of Gracehill Moravian Church. We were warmly received by Reverend Browne in his office in August 2018. He gave words of encouragement for the book and signed a copy of the 250th Anniversary Commemorative Magazine of the Methodist Church. Also in 2018, Serena Christopher was kind enough to show us around the church. Meeting Desmond Thomas while in Antigua in May/June 2022 was an absolute blessing. He took the time to explain the history of the church at Gracefield and also, handed over his own signed copy of a book written by the late Reverend Leon Matthias titled *Gracefield A Northern Star*. Desmond is very passionate about reviving the old historic church located behind the new church, and hopes that one day it will be used as a museum and information centre.

This book is my second publication and is dedicated to the memory of millions of enslaved Africans, who were stolen from their homeland, mistreated and abused on slave ships that forcibly conveyed them to the Americas. Upon their arrival, they were completely stripped of their humanity and forced to work for free on plantations in the Caribbean, North and South American regions. Their anguish and toiling must never be forgotten and may their souls continue to rest in power. For the history enthusiasts, there is so much more to be unearthed in the relationship between the major Christian churches, the institution of slavery and the enslaved Africans, who were clearly victims of the greatest crime against humanity.

Introduction

Antigua (aka: Waladli or Wadadli by the native population) is the largest of the Leeward Islands and the main island of the twin island nation of Antigua and Barbuda. It is famous for its abundant, uncrowded beaches, which are some of the finest in the world. During Britain's colonial domination of the Caribbean region, Antigua was a vital colony due to its excellent harbours and centrality in the north of the Lesser Antilles, its position as the seat of the colonial government of the Leeward Islands, and its role as a major refit station for the British Royal Navy. Further, it was Britain's leading sugar island in the Eastern Caribbean region with almost 200 sugar cane producing mills dotted across the island, making the entire land a sugarcane plantation and factory. In addition, Antigua is littered with many historical churches and chapels. These religious structures were constructed by the four main Christian denominations of the time: Anglican (Church of England), Moravian (aka: Church of the United Brethren), Methodist (aka: Wesleyan) and the Roman Catholic. They are usually referred to as the Older Established Churches and have played a significant role in shaping the social identity and worldview of Antiguan society.

The presence of these powerful religious denominations on Antigua was referenced in an observation made by a Moravian missionary, who did not only label Antigua as a Christian land in 1845, but questioned if there was any Protestant country either in the old or new world, where the population is better supplied by churches and ministers than that of Antigua (Kirton-Roberts, 2015). This bold statement excluded Roman Catholics who, at the time, were legally prevented from practising their faith publicly in Antigua and other British colonies. However, the influence of the Catholic Church in the Americas (aka: New World) was widespread among other major European countries that dominated slavery. According to Catron (2008), Antigua became "the birthplace of Afro-Protestantism in the British Caribbean" and in the early 1800s, it had a significantly higher proportion of Christian converts among the enslaved population than more populated colonies such as Jamaica and Barbados. Antigua was selected to be the subject matter of this book, considering many of its historical firsts. However, the discussions within the book should likewise be seen to a degree as representing the experiences of other Caribbean islands.

The churches built in Antigua by the Older Established Churches between the 1670s and the early 1900s will be the focus of this two-part book. Part One will examine Antigua's history, from its English colonisation to the arrival of Africans. It will also provide an overview of Christianity in Africa prior to the trans-Atlantic slave trade and emphasise the importance of African spiritual practises. In addition, it will look at the history of the four major Christian denominations and their shared relationship with chattel slavery. Furthermore, an attempt will be made to determine why Christianity was introduced to the enslaved population and why those Africans and their children eventually adopted the religion of their enslavers. The book will also explain why European Christians supported the trans-Atlantic slave trade (aka: European slave trade) and the subsequent inhumane treatment of Africans. Other matters to be discussed include apologising for the slave trade, compensation paid to slave owners, and the need for reparations for enslaved descendants. Part two will showcase 24 historic churches and detail their history, congregation establishment, architectural skills and craftsmanship, and the strong influence they had on the religious and social life of the people.

Fundamentally, the book should be read with an open mind, as it is written with the intention of presenting factual information that will decolonise history, and allow the reader to gain a better understanding of the past, as well as to see how some of these actions may have shaped the present. Furthermore, there were a few challenges in writing the book, such as the accuracy of the dates when certain key events occurred. There were also historical records/documents, particularly those pertaining to the Anglican Church, that were not easily accessible in Antigua. Moreover, the reader should be aware that throughout its history, Antigua has been the victim of numerous severe hurricanes, earthquakes and other natural disasters. These disasters have severely damaged many of the island's structures, including many of its historic churches. As a result, it's no surprise that many of these churches have been rebuilt several times.

View from Gracebay Moravian Church, overlooking the Caribbean sea

Part 1

1 Historical Context

The establishment of churches in Antigua started with the arrival of English settlers in 1632. This incursion was sanctioned by the Earl of Carlisle, the legal proprietor, and under warrant from King Charles I of England. It was led by General Sir Thomas Warner, who journeyed with a group of free English and indentured servants from St. Christopher Island (hereafter called St. Kitts), which was founded in 1624 and referred to as the mother colony of the English Caribbean. The settlers in Antigua, like many other English colonies in the Caribbean, came under the protection of the English government and viewed the Anglican Church as a principal source of English national identity. They instituted the Anglican Church as the official State Church and had the services of a cleric as early as 1634, despite the absence of a church building. The planter class, through the authority of the colonial Governors, controlled the Church in Antigua and had the power and influence to dismiss Anglican ministers at will, since they were usually members of the island's all powerful legislature. This was due to the lack of a strong and organised church structure in the British Caribbean.

Race-based chattel slavery was the form of enslavement practised in Antigua, the Caribbean and many other parts of the Americas. It was the worst kind of slavery and meant that enslaved Africans were held as property that could be bought, sold, given away, and inherited. In essence, they and their offspring had no personal rights nor freedom of movement, and were the personal property of the slave owner. The slave owning or planter class could do as they pleased with every aspect of a slave's life and the system of slavery, which was based on cruelty, violence and fear, did not protect the enslaved under the law. From the sixteenth century onwards, this extreme form of chattel slavery became a legalised social institution. In his 1944 book *Capitalism and Slavery*, the Trinidadian scholar and first Prime Minister of Trinidad and Tobago (1961-1981), Dr. Eric Williams explained that "prior to 1783 all classes in English society presented a united front with regard to the slave trade. The monarchy, the Government, the Church, public opinion in general supported the slave trade. There were few protests, and those were ineffective."

Arrival and ill-treatment of enslaved Africans

The introduction of Africans in large numbers to forcibly work as slaves on sugar plantations in Antigua began in the 1670s, when sugar overtook tobacco as the chief crop. This was about three decades after sugar cane production was brought to Barbados by Dutchmen and quickly spread to the Leeward Islands, including Antigua. The Caribbean region initially received just over 30,000 African captives per year. However, this figure grew significantly with the increase of sugar cultivation in the 1700s and reached an average rate of up to 100,000 every year. Enslaved Africans were compelled to work on plantations for six out of the seven day week, with Sunday being their market day and only rest day.

The mortality rate was high, due to overwork, poor nutrition, brutality and disease. It is estimated that one third of the enslaved African population died within the first three years on the plantation and few survived beyond ten years. Moreover, things were so bad in those early times that half of the enslaved women were unable to have children. As a result of the high death rate, European slave merchants continued to import large numbers of African captives to replace those who had died, until the slave trade was abolished in 1807. This practice was captured in a quote by the British poet William Cowper, "I pity them greatly, but I must be mum, for how could we do without sugar or rum?" The high demand for sugar in Europe ensured that the white planter class in the Caribbean were among the wealthiest merchants of the time, even richer than their cousins in the North American colonies.

Entrance to the Barracoon on Nevis Street, St. John's, where enslaved Africans were kept before being sold

During their captivity and after surviving the dreaded Middle Passage (crossing the Atlantic Ocean between Africa and the Americas) where up to 20 percent of captives died in transit, these unfortunate Africans were compelled by European slave-owners and overseers to adapt to new and awful working and living conditions. They had to learn new languages and embrace European values, systems and culture, which was unfamiliar to them. Every enslaved person was compulsorily given a European name and their owner's initials were branded with a hot iron into their skins. Additionally, there was a deliberate policy to separate people of common language and tradition, so as to prevent any form of bonding and the possibility of rebelling. These methods amongst others, were sought to erase the identities of their newly acquired slaves, with a view of breaking their spirits and cutting off any ties with their African past. This prolonged, repressive and inhumane process was referred to as *seasoning* and would usually last anywhere between two to three years. It was simply a case of mental and physical torture.

The labour of enslaved Africans were used to build all of the infrastructures in Antigua and its sister island of Barbuda, including the British Naval Dockyard, over fifty military fortifications around its coastline, plantation houses, windmills, roads and churches. Some enslaved persons worked as blacksmiths, stonemasons, carpenters, and tradesmen, while the majority performed a variety of duties on farms and plantations. For those enslaved labourers (including men, women and children) who worked on sugar plantations, they had to do everything from sowing and harvesting the crops, to the process of turning the extracted sugar cane juice into sugar. This relentless work was generally from sunrise until sunset and averaged about 14 hours a day, six day a week, and during harvest between 16 and 18 hours.

In the Americas, enslaved Africans were intentionally degraded by the system that brutalised and enslaved them. They were labelled as ugly, savages, pagans, heathens, brutes, uncivilised, and a people with no knowledge of Christianity and in need of conversion. Strangely, this negative labelling of Africans came from *civilised* European nations, whose past is tainted with serious human rights abuses and whose own religious practices were once described as pagan, animist and polytheistic. In fact, it was not until the Early Middle Ages (late 5th century to the 10th century) that most of Europe underwent Christianisation.

Christianity in Africa before the trans-Atlantic slave trade

Christianity first came to the continent of Africa via Egypt in the 1st century (around 42 C.E.). In fact, the oldest known manuscript fragment of the New Testament was found in Egypt and dated 125 to 250 C.E. By the 4th century (325 or 328 C.E.), Christianity had become the official state religion of the ancient Kingdom of Axum or Aksum, in what is now Ethiopia (Tigray province) and Eritrea. After Alexandria (present-day Egypt) and Carthage (present-day Tunisia), Ethiopia was the third major centre in early Christian North and Saharan Africa, while Nubia (formerly known as Kush and in present-day Sudan) followed suit during the reign of the Emperor Justinian (527-565 C.E.). Therefore, it can be asserted that the foundation of the early Christian Church was heavily influenced by African philosophers and theologians. Christianity later made further incursions into West and West Central African communities in the 15th century, through the arrival of Portuguese Catholic missionaries, explorers and traders. Actually, the first Christian chapel in West Africa was built within Portugal's first fortress in 1482 at Elmina, a fishing town in today's Ghana.

Meanwhile in 1491, King Nzinga Nkuwu of Kongo Kingdom (aka: Bakongo), a powerful nation in West Central Africa, was baptised as a Christian by Portuguese missionaries and he urged his close family members and Kongo's nobility to follow suit. Incidentally, this was not forced upon him and it occurred a year before Christopher Columbus crossed the Atlantic to the New World. Some observers at the time, saw that the king's conversion was not primarily based on his religious convictions and beliefs, but as a way of sealing the two nation's political and economic ties. Others felt it was based on some compatibility that Christianity had with Kongo cosmology. The conversion led to the emergence of what some scholars have termed as Kongo Christianity, which was a case of Africanising Christianity to fit Kongolese beliefs.

Despite the fact that both systems shared some similar beliefs, such as the practice of exorcism, water baptism, and the existence of one Supreme God, they differed in approaches. Whilst Christian Churches insisted on faith and hope and were bound by sacred texts or scriptures, the various African Spiritual Practices (usually referred to as religions by Europeans) were primarily a non-codified oral tradition and grounded on continuous revelation and getting tangible results. Besides, these spiritual practices are not limited to beliefs in supernatural beings (divinities and spirits) or to ritual acts of worship only; they also taught people how to be self-sufficient and become masters of their own destiny. This proves that the traditional beliefs and practices were intimately connected to the day-to-day lives of the people.

As it happens, many of the men and women transported against their will to the Americas, came from the West Central African region and several West African communities. Some of them, especially those in Kongo and Angola, had already become familiar with Christianity and its teachings. In fact, between the sixteenth and seventeenth centuries well over two million Kongolese had already converted to Catholicism. Moreover, the Portuguese, who were the first Europeans to make inroads into West Africa in 1415, built trading relationships with towns and communities along the coast. One notable example was in 1448, when a Portuguese captain negotiated a peace agreement on behalf of the Portuguese king with important chiefs in the region of Senegambia. This led to the chiefs granting Portugal land to construct a trade fortress. In the 1480s, Portugal received ambassadors from northern and western Africa, including the Kingdom of Kongo and the Jolof Empire. The Kongolese delegation was led by Prince Kasuta and arrived in Lisbon in 1484, where they stayed for one year and half and learnt about Christianity. It was based on their recommendation that the Kongolese elite converted.

Similarly in 1514, the kingdom of Benin (southwestern Nigeria) under the leadership of Oba (king) Ozolua sent his emissaries to Lisbon, while the Portuguese Crown reciprocated by sending Christian missionaries to Benin City. The Benin kingdom was settled by the Edo people, whose civilisation dates back thousands of years and the reign of its first recorded monarchy was in the year 900AD. The Portuguese explorer, Affonso d'Aveiro on reaching Benin in 1486, was astonished how well it was organised and the wealth of the kingdom. He found it comparable to any city in Europe and aptly described it as the great city of Benin. Despite these historical facts, the Portuguese and other European slaving-nations that followed i.e. Spain, France, England/Britain, the Netherlands (Holland), Denmark, Norway and Sweden, still chose to demonise Africans and allowed themselves to be influenced by the huge economic gains that were the main driver behind the trans-Atlantic slave trade. During this *dark* period in history, Africans were referred to as *Black Gold*, since chattel slavery was the iconic capitalist enterprise of its time, just as information technology is today.

African spiritual practices

Before the arrival of the nonconformist Churches (e.g. Moravians, Methodists, Baptists and Presbyterians) in the Americas, many of the enslaved Africans relied on their own customs, spiritual practices and social norms. Although they had some Muslims amongst their ranks, the vast majority practiced African spirituality and used the expertise of priests and healers to deal with spiritual matters and treat various illnesses. The traditional spiritual practices of the African also became a driver in the resistance to slavery and played a significant role in several attempted and successful slave revolts such as the Jamaican Maroon wars (1655-1739), the Prince Klass revolt (1736) in Antigua, Tacky's rebellion in Jamaica (1760) and the Haitian revolution (1791-1804). Many of the enslaved Africans had the belief that their traditional practices gave them spiritual protection. In actual fact, several rebel leaders such as Nanny of the Maroons (Jamaica), and Dutty Boukman and Francois Mackandal of Saint-Domingue (now Haiti) were themselves spiritual leaders.

Consequently, a series of laws were legislated by the European colonists to prevent Africans from practising their tribal, traditional worship and all such practices were made illegal, partly out of fear and to maintain control over the beliefs, values and behaviour of the enslaved Africans. The genesis of such a law was enacted in 1760, as part of a sweeping and repressive act passed in the aftermath of Tacky's Rebellion in Jamaica. The rebellion was the largest of its time (only surpassed by the Haitian Revolution) and lasted several months. From historical accounts, Obeah, which colonial laws described as any assumption of supernatural powers, was considered a serious crime within the British Caribbean and beyond, and punishable by death. However, most territories also provided for alternatives such as transportation (remove the offender from society) and severe floggings.

In many Caribbean colonies, the authorities were concerned that Obeah and other spiritual practices (including the use of drums) played a crucial role in inspiring slave uprisings and other forms of resistance. This may explain why they were firmly against it and passed many anti-Obeah laws, including the Obeah Act, 1904 (Leeward Islands), which applied to Anguilla, Antigua, Barbuda, Montserrat, Nevis, St Kitts, and the British Virgin Islands, and remains the basis of the law in several of these territories (TNA: CO 154/12). Actually, any enslaved person found to be involved in any form of African derived faith such as Candomble (Brazil), Obeah (across the Caribbean), Santeria, Palo or Abakua (Cuba), Shango or Orisha Tradition (Trinidad and Grenada), Winti (Surinam), Myalism/Kumina (Jamaica) or Vodou (Haiti) was brutally punished. Surprisingly, many of these laws, which should have been eradicated during emancipation are still on the statute books of most English speaking Caribbean countries, including Antigua and Barbuda. However, some countries have taken steps to repeal them such as Anguilla (1980), Barbados (1998), Trinidad and Tobago (2000) and St. Lucia (2004).

Christian missionaries and other colonial agents went a step further to label all African spiritual practises as *Satanic*, including referring to African deities or gods as the Devil, or Satan. This was the case with the highly revered indigenous Yoruba deity/Orisha, Esu (aka: Eshu Elegbara) who was redefined, when in reality, his role is to act as an intermediary between Orun (heaven) and Aye (earth). Esu is also a messenger of the oracles and of the Supreme Being, called *Olorun* or *Olodumare* (creator god of the universe). This attempt at associating African deities and spiritual practices with Satan or the Devil is grossly incorrect and was a Euro-Christian construct devised to scare away Africans from their own spirituality, which does not have a character like Satan or the Devil. In the words of an African spiritual practitioner, "Satan is…a foreign concept imported into African societies through colonialism that deliberately sought to stigmatise African spirituality" (Voncujovi, 2020).

Even so, enslaved Africans throughout the Americas found ingenious ways of keeping their rites and rituals alive through stories, dances, songs and folklores (such as the Anansi stories and the Juba dance), and other forms of cultural expression. The fact that these traditional African practices survived the test of time is testament to the effectiveness of cultural resistance. Incidentally, there is today a growing interest amongst African descendants in the Americas to reacquaint themselves with the spiritual/religious practices of their ancestors. It would appear that they are seeking to know the alternative world that their forbears knew existed and for their own self-authentication. According to Erna Brodber (Forde & Paton, 2012): "The colonial powers have been *spirit thieves*. Their obeah legislations have stymied the spiritual growth and development of transported Africans."

Old Gracefield Moravian Church, built by the formerly enslaved and dedicated in August 1839

2 Background of the four main Christian denominations

Anglican

The Anglican Church was created after King Henry VIII (1509–47) decided to break away from the Roman Catholic Church in 1534, due to the Pope's refusal to annul his 23 year old marriage to his first wife Catherine. Subsequently, a law abolishing papal authority in England was passed and Henry was declared Head of the Church of England. On arriving in Antigua and other parts of the Caribbean, the Anglican Church was established to serve English officials and the slave-owning class. Most of its members in those early days supported and, in some cases, participated in the trans-Atlantic slave trade. This was not only confined to Anglicans, but was widely accepted by most Christian Churches (both Catholic and Protestant). In the minds of many early Christians, slavery had been divinely sanctioned. They used parts of the Bible to justify it, while the more seditious parts, like the book of Exodus, the Book of Psalms, and the Book of Revelation were excluded (i.e. in the Slave Bible), so as not to inspire any thoughts of liberation.

Europeans even went as far as to state that Africans had no souls, thereby, suggesting that they were sub-humans, and went on to create a race-based justification for slavery. Subsequently, they passed laws to legitimise the enslavement of Africans such as the Barbados Slave Code of 1661. These were the first set of rules enacted by the British to control and exploit the labour of enslaved Africans, and to establish their status as chattel. Similar slave codes were adopted across British colonies in the Americas, including Antigua and replicated in every European owned colony. These dehumanising slave laws legitimised a state of war between Blacks and Whites, sanctified rigid segregation, and institutionalised an early warning system against slave revolts (Dunn, 1973).

In 1670, the Antigua Council and House of Assembly deemed it necessary to make special provisions for the celebration of marriages on the island and a year later, provision were made to build churches at Falmouth and St. John's. This was for Whites only. The church at Falmouth, St Paul's Anglican, was the first church on Antigua and built in 1671-72. It was a wooden structure and also served as a Court House and Registry. The Church at St John's (capital of Antigua and Barbuda) was likewise built of wood in 1683 and dedicated to St John the Divine. Other Anglican churches began to be erected across the island, after the establishment of five parishes in 1681. With regards to Barbuda, it should be borne in mind that the only historic church established on the island was an Anglican chapel, which was constructed after the visit of Bishop Coleridge in 1825. This is notwithstanding the fact that Barbuda had been colonised two centuries earlier by English settlers from Antigua. The Barbudan chapel is now the Holy Trinity Anglican Church and was erected in 1924. Unfortunately, the church was damaged during Hurricane Irma in 2017 and requires extensive repairs. It is also worth noting that both Methodists and Moravians had a brief presence on Barbuda. The former initiated a mission among the enslaved Africans in 1812, while the latter, visited the island four years later and also began preaching to the same people (Lamport, 2018).

Prior to the emancipation of enslaved Africans in the British Caribbean (starting with Antigua on August 1st, 1834, and most of the other islands on the same date in 1838), the Anglican Church refused to extend any Christian religious rites to people of African descent. This unwillingness of Anglicans to respond to the needs of the enslaved community is well documented. For instance, enslaved Africans were not allowed to attend Anglican Church services, nor could they get married or be buried in the Anglican burial ground. In fact, marriages amongst the enslaved was made illegal under a 1692 law, and only became legal after a uniform marriage code was adopted with the abolition of slavery.

Essentially, the laws of the Church of England prevented Anglican priests from converting the Black population, and the slave system

St John's Anglican Cathedral Church

ensured that they (enslaved or free) were kept out of the Church. In addition, the enslaved were deprived of formal education by the British authorities and slave owners, as this was contrary to both their economic and social interests. However, as public opinion began to change towards slavery in England, the planters were persuaded, for the sake of peace, to tolerate education to some extent. By the mid-1820s organisations like the Society of West India Planters and Merchants (mouthpiece of the pro- slavery lobby), were starting to see the dismantling of slavery as an institution, despite the fact that many of their members (the plantocracy class) refused to accept it. One of the major signs that slavery was on its way out was the introduction of the Amelioration policy of 1823, which was intended to give the enslaved people some protective rights and make the task of Christianising them easier.

The policy made recommendations to improve the treatment of enslaved Africans across British Caribbean colonies, such as allowing and legalising marriages; abolishing Sunday markets while encouraging Christian religious worship on the day; prohibiting family breakup by sale; and limiting the planter's power to punish. The policy became law in June 1824, but was strongly opposed by many planters, who felt that the amelioration agenda was an unfair interference with their property rights. The Church's position on why Amelioration was required was that it was the only way for the Anglican Church to have any real chance of converting enslaved people on a large scale (Painter, J. 2021). As emancipation approached, some planters and their families began to leave the colonies. Due to the continuous migration of their White members back to England, as well as the Anglican missionary effort to Christianise enslaved people, the Anglican Church in Antigua started to soften its stance and began to make a genuine effort to work with the enslaved population. Even after Blacks were allowed to worship in their churches, they were required to sit separately from Whites, thereby discouraging any ideas of equality. This practice continued well into the twentieth century.

In order to ensure greater ecclesiastical discipline, the Anglican Church established two dioceses in the West Indies in 1824: one for Jamaica, which included the Bahamas and Belize, and the other for Barbados, which included the Windward and Leeward Islands and Guyana, with a bishop for each diocese. The year 1825, saw the arrival of the first two bishops in the Caribbean; Christopher Lipscomb (Jamaica) and William Hart Coleridge (Barbados). They brought with them a large contingent of clergies to assist with the Christianisation of the Caribbean's enslaved people. The Diocese of Antigua and the Leeward Islands was established in 1842, and it is now known as the Diocese of the North East Caribbean and Aruba. Other Anglican dioceses formed in the West Indies in the 19th century, included Nassau and the Bahamas, 1861; Trinidad and Tobago, 1872; Windward Islands, 1878; and Honduras (now Belize), 1891.

Nevertheless, as emancipation approached in the early 1830s, the Anglican Church embarked on creating Friendly Societies for the benefit of the enslaved African population and this continued into the post-emancipation and post-abolition years. According to Reverend Robert Robertson (Archdeacon of Antigua from 1843-1850), in 1834, there were eleven Anglican formed societies in Antigua. Many of these societies were designed to assist vulnerable groups such as the elderly, the disabled, and those who were distressed by virtue of poverty. The Anglicans also established Day Schools, which were located on church sites, and prestigious boys' and girls' schools such as Antigua Grammar School for Boys (founded in 1884) and Antigua Girls High School (founded in 1886). Both schools are still in existence to this day.

Moravian

The origins of the Moravian Church (formally Unitas Fratrum or Unity of Brethren), can be traced back to the Roman Catholic priest and Czech reformer Jan (John) Hus (1369-1415), in the fifteenth century Bohemia and Moravia (now Czech Republic). Hus was burned at the stake for heresy, because he objected to some of the practices and doctrines of the Catholic Church and as a result, his followers were bitterly persecuted. With the increase of their persecution in the mid-1600s, Hus' followers were forced to disperse throughout Europe. It was not until 1722 that some members of Unitas Fratrum were given refuge by German nobleman, Count Nicholas Ludwig von Zinzendorf (a devout Lutheran). However, in 1727, Zinzendorf became the leader of the re-established ancient Unitas Fratrum, which became known as the Moravian Church. The Count was responsible for sending the first missionaries outside of Europe to the Danish Caribbean Island of St Thomas in 1732, at the request of Anthony Ulrich, a former enslaved African from St. Thomas who was then living in Copenhagen, Denmark.

The emergence of the Moravian Church to the British Caribbean was made possible, after an Act of Parliament passed by Britain in 1749. The Act recognised the Moravian Church as an ancient Protestant Episcopal Church and secured protection for Moravian missionaries living and working in the British colonies. However, it was not until the arrival of the first Moravian missionary, Englishman Samuel Isles (1723-1764) and his wife on April 1st, 1756 that the Moravian mission officially began in Antigua. It is understood that Isles first preached the gospel to the enslaved under a sandbox tree on the Gambles estate in St John's, which remarkably still stands on the premises to this day. This led to the establishment of the first Moravian station in Antigua, which was called Spring Gardens. In 1762, a small hut was built nearby the *Sandbox Tree* and became the first Moravian Chapel. During the early period of trying to convert the enslaved African community, Samuel Isles faced some challenges such as a lack of money, work, lodging, and most importantly, access to the enslaved Africans that he came to convert. Eventually, Isles was only able to baptise thirty-six Africans before his death in January 1764. It was with the arrival of missionary Peter Braun (also referred to as Brown) in 1769 that

Sandbox tree, Spring Gardens

the Moravian mission in Antigua began to experience a revival and rapid growth in members. In 1771, the church building was enlarged to accommodate the increase in membership. By 1775, the number of Moravian converts in Antigua stood at 2,000.

In his twenty-two years of service in Antigua 1769-91, Peter Braun worked tirelessly and efficiently to manage the affairs of the Moravian church. He connected with the enslaved community by constantly interacting with them. During his ministry, he brought into fruition two more flourishing stations, Bailey Hill (1773) and Gracehill (1781), and helped to increase the total membership to 7,400 members. Around the late 1700s, one fifth of Antigua's black population were Moravians and this increased to half by emancipation in 1834. As a result of this fundamental increase, additional stations were founded such as Lebanon (1837), Five Islands (1838), and Gracefield (1839), which were used to relieve the overgrown congregation at St. John's that was then upwards of 7,000 members.

The further increase in membership was also attributed to the many Black lay pastors and organisers appointed by the church. These *Native Helpers* as they were called, included many women, who assisted in recruiting and instructing the enslaved communities. Additionally, the Moravian church was instrumental in collating the African ethnicities present in Antigua and keeping other valuable records (mostly from 1757-1833) such as names of enslaved people, their baptisms, deaths, their slave-owners' names and, in some cases, their African names and the villages in Africa from where they were kidnapped. Interestingly, the Moravian church registers also highlighted the movements of Afro-Moravians from Antigua to other parts of the Caribbean and North America. Even though Moravians evangelised actively among enslaved Africans, they also played a part in convincing many of them, especially those born in Africa to forego their African customs and cultural identities.

Westerby Memorial, St John's

Before emancipation, prejudices against enslaved people learning to read subsided marginally and the Moravians at this point were running day and evening schools out of every station and other temporary buildings. As a result of a policy decision taken in 1825 to erect school houses, the Moravians had completed two of such schools at its Gracehill and Newfield stations by 1827. After emancipation on August 1, 1834, the Moravian church expanded its work in educating the newly freed slaves and constructed additional schools, including a training school for young Female Teachers' at Sea View Farm (Lebanon) in 1840, which later moved to St John's (Spring Gardens) in 1854, and a Boys' Training School that relocated from Lebanon in 1846 to Jennings Village (Cedar Hall) in 1847. By 1868 the Moravian Church was operating several schools in Antigua, but were forced to hand over running most of these schools to the government, because of the economic crisis that preceded the First World War (1914-1918) and the cut in government educational grants.

Towards the end of the twentieth century, the Moravian Church became involved in running pre-school education, something they have continued to the present day. Apart from the education of its members, Moravians also catered for their welfare and established friendly societies at Spring Gardens, Gracehill, Newfield, Gracebay, Lebanon and Cedar Hall. These organisations provided acts of benevolence to its members and the under privilege in society. Moreover, young people and adults were encouraged to join several church groups and ministries such as prayer meeting groups, bible study groups, youth/senior choirs, Kings Daughters Circle, Youth Fellowship, Women's and Men's fellowships. These groups became a source of spiritual enhancement to members of the church.

Methodist

The Methodist movement was founded in the 18th century by Anglican priests, John Wesley and his brother Charles, and other members of the *Holy Club* at Oxford University. The group was dedicated to the reading of scripture and carried out their Christian faith methodically. This is the reason for their name; the Methodists. However, their vision was to revive the Church of England and not to create a new church. What later emerged was a breakaway sect that disagreed with the theology, liturgy, and polity of the Church of England and refused to submit to its authority.

John and Charles Wesley's spiritual journey was inspired by Moravians. This happened during their voyage to the colony of Georgia, U.S.A in 1735, after John noticed the calm nature of some German Moravians when a storm struck the ship. While other passengers were scared, the Moravians were calmly singing and praying. John was moved by their certainty of faith and decided to have discussions with Moravian Pastors on his return to England. The brothers' interactions with Moravians became instrumental in their spiritual awakening in May 1738, as they now had a new understanding of what it meant to have an unshakable faith in God. This led to their conversion in which, they committed to seek Christ alone for their salvation. John Wesley preached the gospel extensively and structured a movement which became the origin of the Methodist Church; while Charles is noted to have written thousands of hymns, many of which are still sung widely today.

The Methodist congregation in Antigua believed that Methodism came to Antigua by the grace of God. The experience of Nathaniel Gilbert, who was responsible for introducing Methodism to Antigua in 1760, affirms this and, therefore, makes Antigua the first Methodist missionary station outside of Britain. He was a British slave plantation owner, lawyer and Speaker of the Antigua House of Assembly. Nathaniel Gilbert was also one of the four judges appointed by the legislature to investigate the 1736 (Prince Klaas) conspiracy. While recovering from a brief illness in 1756, Gilbert read a pamphlet sent to him by his brother, Francis Gilbert. The pamphlet, titled *An Appeal to Men of Reason and Religion*, was authored by John Wesley and became a turning point in his life.

In 1757 a year after recuperating, Nathaniel Gilbert embarked on a two year journey to England with his family and three enslaved household servants, Mary Alley, Sophia Campbell and Bessie, with the purpose of meeting John Wesley. After meeting and hearing Wesley preach in London in 1758, it is believed that Nathaniel, his wife, and servants converted to Methodism. Wesley actually baptised both Sophia Campbell and Mary Alley. On returning to Antigua, Nathaniel Gilbert began preaching the Gospel to enslaved Africans from his estate, on the back steps of his plantation house. This became the first Methodist pulpit in the Caribbean. Gilbert faced numerous challenges, as one would expect in a society where slavery was an accepted institution. In 1766, the first Methodist Society in the Caribbean was established in Antigua.

With the growth of Methodism in Antigua, Nathaniel Gilbert decided to relinquish his position as the Speaker of the House of Assembly and dedicated more time to this work. By the time of his death on April 20th, 1774, the Methodist Society of Antigua numbered 200 members. After Nathaniel's death, his brother Francis, who had returned to Antigua just before his brother's death, took on the responsibility for maintaining Methodism in Antigua. However, due to ill health, Francis returned to England in 1776 and died three years later. In the absence of an appointed leader, the Methodist movement in Antigua faced tremendous challenges, but was kept alive by Sophia Campbell, a Negress, and Mary Alley, a Mulatto, until the arrival of John Baxter, a shipwright and local preacher from Chatham, England in 1778. The role of these women and many others who flocked to the church and preached the gospel message to other fellow enslaved persons, encouraged many to become Methodist. Unfortunately, these women and many others who led and grew the Methodist Society in their local areas, were refused leadership positions across the Caribbean by the Methodist hierarchy. Nonetheless, the contributions of Sophie Campbell and

Monument located at the Gilbert centre to commemorate the beginnings of Methodism in 1760

Mary Alley was acknowledged by Baxter and may have helped to influence his determination and drive to spread Methodism in Antigua.

During the end of his first year, John Baxter had increased the Methodist congregation to six hundred. Under his leadership and the benevolence of Mrs Francis Gilbert (Francis's widow) and others, the first Methodist Chapel in Antigua and the Caribbean was erected in 1783, on Tanner Street, St. John's. The Chapel was a wooden structure with a seating capacity of 2,000 people. The growth of Methodism in Antigua was further enhanced by the presence of Dr. Thomas Coke, a notable Methodist missionary leader, who landed in Antigua on Christmas morning of 1786, in the company of the first missionaries to the Caribbean. This was after his ship was diverted by storms on its way to Halifax, Nova Scotia, Canada. Upon arrival, Coke and three young preachers walked towards St. John's and met Baxter who was on his way to morning service. After a little refreshment, they all proceeded to the Methodist chapel, where Coke read prayers, preached, and administered the Sacrament to the congregation. The congregation of 2,000 members, comprised of enslaved Africans and a small number of white Methodist settlers. Dr. Coke was pleased with his short stay in Antigua and preached twice a day in St. John's. By 1788, the Methodists membership had reached 3,000.

Like the Moravians, Methodists gave priority to the education and welfare needs of their members. Though, much of the education provided by the main Christian denominations, especially prior to emancipation, was not designed to promote independent critical thought, but was generally basic and delivered orally. Nonetheless, the Methodists led the way by starting the first Sunday school in the Caribbean at English Harbour in 1809, and erected the first schoolroom for educating the enslaved African population at Bethesda in 1813. The schoolroom was the first of its kind in the English speaking Caribbean and was the initiative of an enslaved man, Vigo Blake. The building was called *Bethesda* by Mrs. Thwaites, a free-coloured Antiguan Methodist, whose husband Charles, an English Methodist, taught at the school. Bethesda was not the only place where the Methodist built schools. According to the Inspector of Schools report (1887), the Wesleyans operated a number of day schools across Antigua. These schools and those of other denominations were taken over by the government, after they assumed responsibility for public education in 1914. However, the religious organisations continued to influence the educational landscape. The Methodists also assisted with the establishment of free villages built by the formerly enslaved such as Freemansville and Bethesda, and initiated various social outreach programmes to support its members.

Sign board located at the site of the first school in the British Caribbean

Roman Catholic

The Roman Catholic Church is the origin of all major Christian denominations in Europe. In fact, Catholicism has been the spiritual power that underpins the history of Western civilization. The role of the Roman Catholic Church since the very beginning of the slave trade in 1441, has been somewhat conflicting and described by some scholars as complex. On the one hand, it is believed that the Church was culpable in the enslavement of Africans during the trans-Atlantic slave trade, since the edicts or papal bulls enacted by Catholic Popes played a central role in their capture and enslavement. This was seen as the reason that the Catholic Church did not fervently oppose the institution of slavery, but simply played lip service to a system that economically enriched the Church. On the other hand, supporters of the Catholic Church have claimed that the Church had consistently condemned the practice of chattel slavery and it was individual Catholics who supported slavery or owned slaves. Notwithstanding these claims and counterclaims, the inhumane trafficking of Africans continued unabated.

Catholics have been resident in colonial Antigua almost from its inception. They were the Irish who came to Antigua and other English colonised Caribbean islands as indentured servants, prisoners of war and merchants. The Leeward Islands census taken in 1678 showed that Antigua had 610 Irish people out of a population of 4480. Before the Catholic Emancipation Act of 1829, Catholics in Antigua could face prosecution if found practising their faith publicly. In an area popularly known today as Pope's Head Street in St. John's, the English people would behead the image of the Pope every year and burn it. The castigation of Catholics originated from laws passed in England in 1534 and 1559, when English monarchs were declared as Head of the Church in England and no longer the Pope in Rome. These laws and many others that followed, deprived Catholics of their rights in Britain and throughout its colonies.

Catholicism in Antigua found a voice through Countess Sarah Masterson, owner of the Blake estate. Her religious affiliation was an exception for plantation owners, since most were Anglicans. The Countess was a passionate Roman Catholic who regularly wrote to the Bishop of Roseau in Dominica (Catholics in Antigua were under his jurisdiction at the time), requesting for the service of a priest to meet the spiritual needs of Catholics in Antigua. In 1859, Antigua received its first resident Catholic priest, a Father J. Ryan. This was prompted by the earlier arrival of about 2,000 Portuguese indentured workers mainly from Madeira, all of whom were Roman Catholics. They were later followed by other Catholic immigrants from Lebanon and Syria. In recent times, the Catholic population in Antigua has been further increased by migrants from Dominica and the Dominican Republic. The intervention and persistency of Countess Masterson to develop the Catholic Church in Antigua was incredible. She did everything necessary to bring this into fruition, including donating land for the construction of a chapel. Her tenacity was mentioned in the famous Antiguan book, *To Shoot Hard Labour*, where the narrator Samuel Smith (aka: Papa Sammy) recounted a story by his mother, about how Countess Masterson gave food to people in exchange for worshiping at the Catholic Church.

Antigua's first Roman Catholic Church was erected in 1869, at the corner of Church Street and Independence Avenue (formerly East Street). Prior to its construction, Catholics in Antigua met at two locations, a two storied house on lower Redcliffe Street and a building on Lower North Street near the Point. The first church was later replaced by a new and bigger church, owing to its small size and the discovery of some structural weaknesses. The new church was built in 1909 and named St Joseph's and St Patrick's Catholic Church. With the creation of the Diocese of St. John's-Basseterre in 1971 (covering five English-speaking jurisdictions in the Caribbean, including Antigua and Barbuda), the church became a pro-Cathedral (a parish church used as a cathedral). In 1981, Bishop Donald James Reece was ordained and he began plans for a new cathedral. The magnificent structure named Holy Family Cathedral was completed in 1987. As a Co-Cathedral, the Holy Family Church shares the seat of the bishop with the Immaculate Conception in Basseterre, St. Kitts, however, the official residence of the bishop is in St. John's, Antigua.

First Roman Catholic Chapel, Lower Redcliffe Street, St. John's

The religious congregations within the Catholic Church in Antigua focused its work in areas of education and social work. Through the St. Vincent de Paul Society, numerous worthwhile projects were initiated such as The Good Shepherd Home for Abused and Abandoned Girls, and several others to support the elderly. Also, the Church works alongside other Christian denominations in Antigua and are active members of both the Antiguan Christian Council and the Caribbean Council of Churches. The Catholics were also responsible for building two of Antigua's most renowned schools, Christ the King High School (1933) and St. Joseph's Academy (1958).

3 The connection between European Christianity and the Trans- Atlantic Slave Trade

According to historians, there are numerous evidence to confirm that Christian Churches (including the pacifists Quakers) actively participated in the slave trade, as majority of early Christian leaders held the view that slavery was consistent with Christian theology. The genesis of this ideology can be found in the papal bulls issued in 1452 (Dum Diversas), 1455 (Romanus Pontifex) and 1493 (Inter Caetera). The edict of 1452, which was issued by Pope Nicholas V, granted King Alfonso of Portugal (and his successors) permission to "conquer Saracens (Muslims), pagans and other infidels and enemies of Christ" in West Africa and beyond, and put them into perpetual slavery and take all their lands, possessions and properties. As a result, the same pope's 1455 bull was used to justify the expansion of (Black) African slavery within early Iberian colonies (Spain and Portugal), as well as the acquisition of more African captives and territory.

Nonetheless, it was the bull of 1493, issued by Pope Alexander VI that gave Spain and Portugal the authority to colonise, convert and enslave the indigenous people of Africa, Asia, Australia, New Zealand and the Americas. In essence, the world was divided into two parts with Portugal granted sovereignty to territories in the East and Spain given the exclusive right to discover and colonise the West (aka: The Americas or New World). In addition, the concept of claiming lands owned and occupied by indigenous non-Christian people (aka: Doctrine of Discovery), promoted European Christian dominance and was driven by White supremacy ideology. Further, it was the emergence of these various papal bulls that signalled to the rest of Christian Europe that the enslavement of Africans during the trans-Atlantic slave trade was acceptable and justified. Interestingly, it was the Spanish Dominican Catholic priest and former conquistador, Bartolome de Las Casas (1484-1566) who in 1518, advocated for the importation of Africans to work as slaves in the Americas. He believed that Africans, as opposed to indigenous (native) Americans, were naturally suited to forced labour and enslavement. Basically, the Spaniards believed that one African was worth four Native Americans, and de Las Casas' suggestion horribly changed the course of history for Black Africans and exemplified the Church's hypocrisy.

Christian Churches and the trans-Atlantic slave trade

Further evidence revealed that many leaders of the major Christian denominations were also involved in the dreadful institution of slavery. For example, the Jesuits (aka: the Society of Jesus), a prominent order of Catholic priests, were major slaveholders who relied on the labour of enslaved Africans on their sugar plantations in Spanish, Portuguese and British America. Some leading clergymen openly expressed their opposition to the slave trade's abuses, however their intention was not to stop the enslavement of Africans, but to ensure that the enslaved were treated with some humanity. An example of such a cleric was George Whitefield, a popular Anglican evangelist and one of the founders of Methodism. Although he originally spoke out fervently against the cruelty of many slave owners in the American colonies, he later used biblical arguments to defend and support slavery, and even went on to accept enslaved Africans gifted to him in Georgia, USA. This paradoxical view was not limited to members of a particular Christian denomination, but was spread across all denominations.

Another example of this double standard was expounded by the Society for Propagating the Gospel (SPG), today USPG, an overseas missionary branch of the Anglican Church. In 1710, they were bequeathed two sugar plantations and 300 slaves on the death of Christopher Codrington, the Barbadian planter and former Governor-General of the Leeward Islands. After running the sugar plantations in Barbados as brutal as any commercial slave owner for 120 years, the SPG relinquished its slaveholdings in 1833 and were compensated to the tune of £8,823 (almost £1 Million today), under the Slavery Abolition Act (1833). According to Church Times online newspaper, a groundbreaking research by University College London (UCL) found that almost 100 Church of England clergy received financial compensation after slavery was abolished. The total amount is said to be equivalent to £46 million in today's money (Wyatt, 2020).

One more historical evidence that corroborates the Church's involvement and participation in this economic/business venture was their presence at slave ports such as Elmina Castle (aka: Elmina Slave Dungeon) and numerous other forts and castles both on the Gold Coast (modern day Ghana) and across Africa. Many Christian denominations have been accused of collaborating with European slave merchants and saw nothing wrong with building churches on top of dungeons, where captives were languishing to death. This relationship between slavery and the Christian church was reiterated by the British historian Hugh Thomas, who claimed that all the Christian denominations were strongly involved in the slave trade (Thomas, 1997).

In reality, it was not until the end of the 18th century that churches and religious leaders began to openly condemn chattel slavery. This new mind-set led to a drastic change, which brought about the establishment of the Society for Effecting the Abolition of the Slave Trade in 1787. The Society comprised of British abolitionists such as Thomas Clarkson, Granville Sharp and William Wilberforce, who were trying to raise public awareness and lobby for the abolition of the slave trade. The first speech on this issue by Wilberforce (Member of Parliament for Hull) to the British Parliament was in 1789, and he used the report of a Moravian Brethren to support his argument. This report had strongly advocated that the Moravian methods of work was found to move the enslaved population away from rebellion and made them "fit for the great gift of liberty" (Hutton, 1909). Paradoxically, it was Britain that became the world's leading slave-trading country for more than two centuries (prior to the 1780s), and also produced some of the most famous abolitionists.

Evangelical Revival and the abolition of slavery

From around the mid-1700s during the Evangelical Revival or First Great Awakening (1730s and 1740s), religious groups such as the Moravian and Methodist conceived a new perspective to ease the burden of slavery for the enslaved, without jeopardising the planter's position of power. This new outlook was not to place Africans as equals, but to gain the approval of slave owners, who were resistant about Christianising enslaved Africans, since they believed that conversion would not only challenge the colonial social order of *master* and *slave*, but could incite unrest and rebellion on the part of the enslaved. So, the missionaries tried to reassure slave owners and the White population that by converting enslaved Africans to Christianity, they would become more obedient, hardworking and loyal, which would solidify the planters' power. Fundamentally, this was a tireless effort to bring some change to the cruel condition on the plantations, without really abolishing slavery. Consequently, enslaved men and women were indoctrinated by Christian missionaries to accept their confined and submissive state, while also being taught to obey their masters. Being disobedient to him or her implied disobedience to God. This view was echoed in the 1821 report of the Methodist Missionary Society, where it was mentioned that "the Methodists were being accepted because they were helping to keep the increasingly restless slaves quiet by giving them a more divine purpose to live for." (Olwig, 1990).

Even the founder of the Moravian Mission in Europe, Count Von Zinzendorf, who firmly believed in slavery, had this to say to a group of enslaved persons in St. Thomas (1739): "God punished the first Negroes by making them slaves, and your conversion will make you free, not from the control of your masters, but simply from your wicked habits and thoughts, and all that makes you dissatisfied with your lot." It was this type of missionary rhetoric that was used to convince many within the enslaved community to look for their reward in heaven, which in turn, reassured slave owners that it was safe to give protestant missionaries access to preach to enslaved Africans on their plantations. Once it was identified that conversion would quell any form of agitation, slave owners began to encourage enslaved Africans to convert to Christianity and in some cases, donated land for a place of worship to be built. In Antigua, many of the planters were particularly drawn to Moravian missionaries, whose methods of work was thought to teach enslaved Africans to be industrious, orderly and loyal (Hutton, 1909).

Conversion of enslaved Africans to Christianity

The conversion of enslaved Africans from their own traditional practices to European Christianity may be perplexing to many observers, as it was the religion of their oppressors and abusers. However, the reason why Christianity was ultimately embraced was influenced by a number of different factors. According to some scholars these included sheer survival, finding protection from the menacing slave masters, an opportunity to become organised and obtain basic education, re-establishing social relations with long lost kinsmen and women, hearing the message of salvation from a Black convert, believing that baptism equates freedom and the Bible's stance on freedom, equality and justice.

Catron (2008) further argues that Antigua's political economy, the actions of certain Black and White evangelicals, the island's geography and the yearning for stability by people of African descent, played vital and intersecting roles in bringing about Christian conversion. Interestingly, Lois Rothe (a Danish public official), on a post emancipation visit to Antigua in 1845, stated that within a decade after emancipation, Christian missionaries had successfully converted thousands of Africans to Christianity. This was achieved with the support of the main Christian denominations, financial donors such as the Christian Missionary Society (CMS), Lady Mico Charity, the British colonial government and former slave owners. It should be noted that at this time in Antiguan history, the enslaved population showed preference to the Moravian and Methodist Churches, rather than the established Anglican Church.

Therefore, it can be deduced that Christianity was used to foster loyalty, inculcate discipline, encourage assimilation, change behaviour and integrate the formerly enslaved Africans and their descendants into a system that did not threaten the colonial order. Consequently, the Christian indoctrination of Africans during the period of slavery and afterwards, contributed immensely to the eradication of many traditional African beliefs and practices. Yet, it was the indigenous beliefs, values and cultural expressions of Africans that influenced and shaped, to a large extent, the form of Christianity that emerged. This was a new hybrid religion, which blended some *African* with Christian beliefs. Even though Christianity eventually played a pivotal role in the abolition of slavery and the slave trade, it did not fulfil the promise of equality and true freedom that was accorded to Whites. Instead, the lives of the formerly enslaved was riddled with poverty and exploitation, and they were forced to make the best out of a bad situation. Hence, the legacy of Christianity as a beacon of hope, remains tainted by its silence, activities and entanglement in the trading and enslavement of Africans.

Apology and reparation for the slave trade

Over the past decades, some Christian denominations such as Catholics, Anglicans, Presbyterians, Quakers and Baptists have admitted to being involved in the trans-Atlantic slave trade and some have apologised. The Church of England's apology was prompted by the severity of its complicity and may explain why its Synod unanimously voted to apologise for slavery. Their collective sentiment was echoed in the words of Reverend Simon Blessant of Blackburn: "we (the Church) were at the heart of it (the slave trade). We were directly responsible for what happened. In the sense of inheriting our history, we can say we owned slaves, we branded slaves, that is why I believe we must actually recognise our history and offer an apology" ("Church apologises for slave trade," 2006). In the same general Synod meeting held in 2006, the Right Reverend Butler, the Bishop of Southwark, highlighted that "bishops in the House of Lords with biblical authority voted against the abolition of the slave trade" and that "the profits of the slave trade were part of the bedrock of our country's industrial development; no one who was involved in running the business, financing it or benefiting from its products can say that they had clean hands" (Zacek, 2013).

Subsequently, for these apologies to be meaningful, the entire Christian Church owes it to the enslaved Africans in assisting to eliminate the legacies of slavery and the institutionalised racism that emerged out of it. According to Eric Williams in his book *Capitalism & Slavery*, "Slavery was not born of racism, rather racism was the consequence of slavery." Therefore, the call for reparations from the descendants of the formerly enslaved should not be ignored, but seen as an urgent necessity worthy of attention. Moreover, slavery is not something you can simply apologise for and deemed the matter closed. Whilst Africans enslaved in the New World were clearly the victims of this cruel act and received no form of recompense, the British government paid out an immense sum of £20 million compensation to 46,000 British slave-owners for the loss of property in people. The amount borrowed came from a syndicate organised by Nathan Mayer Rothschild (Donington, 2014) and it is estimated to be worth tens of billions of pounds in today's money.

Additionally, the University College London's (UCL) Centre for the Study of the Legacies of British Slave-ownership research found that compensation was not only paid to rich families, but also, to many ordinary people. This has ignited further discussions that shows how slavery contributed significantly to Britain's economy, society, polity and culture. Actually, the money used to compensate slave owners represented a staggering 40 percent of the UK government's total annual budget or about 5 percent of its Gross Domestic Product (GDP). In a BBC documentary article featured in the Guardian online newspaper in July 2015, it was mentioned that the amount was the largest bailout in British history until the bailout of the banks in 2009. Incidentally, the loan was only paid off by the British tax payers in 2015. Ironically, the descendants of those enslaved people resident in the UK, were also made to contribute to the payment of the said sum through taxation.

In recent years, the call for reparations has grown louder. The British government in responding to that call in August 2020, stated that "the UK deplores the human suffering caused by slavery and the slave trade. They are among the most abhorrent chapters in the history of humanity." However, this statement fell short of Britain taking full responsibility for the atrocious part it played during the trans-Atlantic slave trade and for the UK government to then declare that "reparations are not part of the government's approach", is not only shameful, but extremely offensive. Even a speech in 1789 to the British Parliament by the abolitionist, William Wilberforce, reminded the lawmakers to reflect on centuries of British exploitation of Africa and how they have degraded Africans, without any consideration of guilt. He alluded that Parliament should not be insensitive to the principles of national justice and called for reparations to be made to Africa, whilst establishing trade based on true commercial principles.

Conclusion

There is no denying that the main Christian denominations discussed in this book, remain at the centre of community life in Antigua and Barbuda. Yet, there is ample evidence that the Church as a whole was also complicit in the trans-Atlantic slave trade, as well as the annihilation of many indigenous civilisations. Furthermore, during the period known as the Age of Discovery (15th-17th century), they imposed Christianity on these cultures. It was an era when Christianity was spread throughout the world as a result of missionary work. Some observers studying the same period believe that Christianity was used as a possible military weapon of invasion, because it was spread through conquest and enslavement. According to historian John Henrik Clarke, European nationalism has dominated this planet for the past 500 centuries. Europe has always believed in one thing: European dominance, whether it be under the guise of Capitalism, Socialism, Fascism, or Christianity.

In the case of Africans, Europeans saw nothing wrong in demonising their spiritual or religious practices and referring to them by a variety of derogatory names. They mocked African customs and spread lies and misinformation to keep millions of enslaved Africans and their descendants from ever knowing or learning anything positive about their African roots. Despite their efforts to associate Christian conversion with civility and the abolition of slavery, it did not stop the exploitation and cruelty meted out to black Africans. Contrary to popular belief, the majority of the people in the countries that participated in the trans-Atlantic slave trade are no longer Christians. They may describe themselves as Christian nations, but many of their citizens now identify as Atheists and non-religious.

The trans-Atlantic slave trade was certainly a lucrative business that provided wealth for the Church, various European royal families, European nation-states, New World colonies and numerous individuals. It was strictly an economic venture that ignored morality and was justified on every count. In fact, the British and other European slave trading nations including the United States of America (U.S.A), used the huge profits, patterns of trade and systems of work derived from the slave trade to develop and drive the industrial revolution that began in the early 1800s. When it comes to the role of Christian missionaries during slavery, it is clear that they were more concerned with winning souls, rather than change the laws that condemned millions of enslaved Africans to a life of servitude. In addition, the missionaries developed friendly relationships with slave-owners, and were praised for their ability to impose a set of European-derived behavioural norms on the enslaved and formerly enslaved population. Any violation of these standards would be considered un-Christian behaviour. In short, Christianity was allegedly used as a form of social control.

While it may be desirable for the descendants of slaveholders and some other Europeans who benefit from *White privilege* to tell those descended from enslaved Africans to *get over it* or *move on* from slavery, it is naive for them to expect that over 400 years of injustice and genocide should simply be brushed aside. Such utterances are insensitive, disrespectful and blatantly disingenuous, considering that millions of Africans were stolen from their homes, stripped of their names, languages, history, traditions, beliefs, spirituality and cultural heritage. To this day, African descendants have continued to experience gross inequality, racial discrimination and a lack of social mobility. Although, a small fraction of the descendants of slave owners are making some effort at atonement, and certain institutions such as banks and universities have owned up to their part in slavery, it is now left with the governments of former slave-owning countries (i.e. the United States, United Kingdom, France and others) to take the bold decision to offer a resounding apology and pay the long overdue reparations to the descendants of enslaved Africans, many of whom still carry the pain and the scars of their ancestors.

While slave-owners were the main beneficiaries of the compensation process, the newly freed Africans received absolutely nothing for their labour and were left to fend for themselves. After receiving the generous pay out legislated in the Slavery Abolition Act of 1833, slave owners in Antigua were still able to sell part of their estate (landed property) to the government. For these people, it was a win-win situation. With all of these unjust benefits and what is known about how these plantation or estate owners mistreated and brutalised enslaved Africans, it is ironic that the majority of Antiguan villages still bear their names. There is no doubt that the communities of churches, which were themselves guilty, have an obligation to take over and begin correcting past wrongs. They have to start by teaching their congregation the truth about the Church's history with slavery. Furthermore, in order to address its links to colonialism and slavery, the Church must take decisive action to pay its own share of reparations. The impact of the trans-Atlantic slave trade, which spanned from Canada to Argentina, remains an open wound within these communities and must be addressed urgently, so as to promote the necessary healing that will bring about the much-needed closure to this historical injustice.

The historical churches scattered throughout the landscape of Antigua should be considered as an integral part of the history of the nation of Antigua and Barbuda. Although, their influences may have somewhat diminished and their congregations declining, they remain as reminders of the sacrifice, strength, courage and perseverance of those enslaved men and women, countless of whom laboured day and night to construct many of these churches. Their commitments to establish and sustain church congregations that supported local communities must be honoured. Further, homage should be paid to them as victims of the world's greatest crime against humanity, and recognition given to the day they got their freedom - August 1, 1834 (Emancipation Day). This day should be one of remembrance, reflection, joy and celebration. Failure to enact this historic event will expose generations of young people to a future without a foundation.

The significance of remembering emancipation celebrations and the history of slavery was highlighted in an interview with the late Dr. Rev. Wycherley Gumbs (Anguillian Methodist Minister), which was later published as a document in 2007. Dr Gumbs emphasised the importance of teaching children about slavery, its abuses and oppression. He also suggested that schools and families should start participating in emancipation celebrations, and hope that governments would integrate them in the education curriculum at every level. He concluded that "if we fail to instruct our children and integrate the emancipation theme in our culture, we are condemning them to be like driftwood on the ocean without direction, and to be at the mercy of every whim and fashion which are prevalent in the culture."

Therefore, based on what has been discussed in this book, it is for these reasons that the historical churches of Antigua ought to be preserved for posterity.

*"There is no more powerful force than a people steeped in their history. And there is no higher cause than honoring our struggle and ancestors by remembering." - Dr. Carter Godwin Woodson (Author: **The Mis-Education of the Negro**).*

Our Lady of the Valley Anglican Church, Dedicated September 1689

Part 2

4 Historical Churches of Antigua

Antigua can boast of many historical churches, as stated on the introductory page. Some of these churches, dating from the 16th century, were among the island's oldest, strongest and most impressive buildings. The reasons why some of the churches were considered unique, was due to the type of materials used in their construction, as well as the tremendous architectural skills and craftsmanship. Many of these beautiful churches have been carefully restored, preserved and survived centuries of earthquakes and hurricanes. Today, they form part of the idyllic landscape of the twin island nation of Antigua and Barbuda, and several churches are still actively used as a place of worship.

Many of the fascinating churches that will be presented in this section of the book, became centres of religious and social life and had strong influences on some of the independent settlements or free villages that emerged in Antigua after emancipation. For example, Anglicans had sway over Bendals, Cedar Grove and All Saints, while the Methodist churches were influential in Bethesda, English Harbour, Sawcolts and Freetown. But it was the Moravians who had the greatest influence and were well established in Old Road, Newfield, Liberta, Sea View Farm, Swetes, Five Islands and Greenbay. It is also worth noting that Anglican churches were typically constructed far away from plantations, whereas Moravian and Methodist churches were built close to enslaved communities. In certain cases, the congregations existed well before the church was built.

A total of 24 historic churches were chosen to be featured (Anglican: 8; Moravian: 8; Methodist: 6; Roman Catholic: 2), including aspects of their history, the founding and endurance of their congregations, and several beautiful photos of these magnificent structures. Furthermore, it is anticipated that the information shared about these must-see churches will be appealing to all visitors as well as Antiguans and Barbudans.

Anglican

St Paul's Anglican Church

St. Paul's Anglican Church is located in the historic town of Falmouth, St. Paul Parish. Falmouth was the first town in Antigua and site of the first parish church called St Paul's. The church was a wooden structure constructed between 1671 and 1672. It was also used as a courthouse by the early English settlers. In the area of education, St. Paul's started three schools for children of the plantocracy with the first built in the late 1670's, which was a Chapel School called St. Barnabas. The other two schools were in Falmouth and English Harbour. The original St. Paul's church was destroyed by the massive earthquake of 1843. This was followed by the laying of a cornerstone on the same site on January 15th, 1847 and the new church was opened for worship on February 6th, 1858. This church was later damaged by lightning in July 1880, and what remained of it was completely destroyed by Hurricane Dog on 31 August, 1950.

The current St. Paul's Anglican Church was rebuilt on the foundation of the old church in 1952. One of the colonial-era tombstones in the churchyard belongs to Colonel Phillip Warner, Governor of Antigua (1674-75), who died in 1689. Another notable tomb is that of James Charles Pitt, son of a former Prime Minister of the United Kingdom, who was buried in the courtyard in 1780. In 1816, St. Paul's began the baptising and burying of free coloured people and members of the enslaved community. Further, the church established a Female Refuge Society at English Harbour and a soup kitchen in the 1830s. St. Paul's Anglican Church is a significant historic landmark that continues to serve the local community today.

St. Barnabas Anglican Church

St. Barnabas Anglican Church was a Chapel School and a Chapel of Ease from the late 1670s to 1843. It is located in the village of Liberta, St. Paul Parish. Liberta, meaning *liberty or freedom,* was one of the very first free villages founded in 1835 by the newly freed Africans. Like the mother church of St Paul's in Falmouth, the original St. Barnabas was a wooden structure. After many decades of continuous use, the building began to show signs of disrepair and a programme of reconstruction commenced between 1824 and 1842. The new stone building was constructed with red bricks and locally sourced Antigua green stone.

This charming little church was consecrated as a place of worship for the congregation across the parish, after the parish church of St. Paul's was destroyed by the earthquake of 1843 and was temporarily out of use. As a result of an increase in its congregation and over a century and a half of constant use, St Barnabas eventually underwent extensive restoration work in 1989,

while maintaining the original Italianate architectural design and was rededicated on Sunday 10th December, 1989. The historic St. Barnabas is an extremely small chapel and seats between 50-75 persons. It is one of the most photographed churches in Antigua and worth a stop on the way to English Harbour.

St. George's Anglican Church

The first St. George's Chapel was erected in 1687 at Fitches Creek. It became a Chapel of Ease to St Peter's Church in Parham, as the Parish of St. George was originally part of St. Peter Parish. After the new parish of St. George was created in 1725, the chapel with its burial ground was upgraded to a parish church. In 1735, St. George's Church was enlarged, but it was severely damaged by the 1843 earthquake and a series of hurricanes, particularly two consecutive ones in 1950. The second hurricane destroyed almost all of the wattle and daub houses (low income housing) on the island, and left the vast majority of Antiguans homeless. The cost of the damage was estimated to be around $1 million USD (approx. 12 Million USD today).

St. George's underwent extensive restoration work over a fifteen year period, which was completed in 1965. After Hurricane Luis made landfall in Antigua in 1995, the church underwent additional restoration and expansion work. All physical damage caused by the hurricane to the church building was repaired, and the church was rededicated in 2001. St. George's Anglican Church is located in Fitches Creek and has a beautiful view of the Creek and Parham Harbour. It is also a popular location for romantic weddings.

Our Lady Of The Valley Anglican Church

Our Lady of the Valley Anglican Church is one of the few historic churches in Antigua dating from the late 1600s. The Valley Church, as it is commonly known, was dedicated in September 1689 and is named after the Valley Church Bay Beach and Valley Road. It is located in Bolans Village, St. Mary Parish, which is situated on the south-west part of Antigua. The village use to be a farming community, but has been transformed into a centre of tourist activity. It is home to some of the best beaches on the island.

Our Lady of the Valley Anglican Church is a beautiful church, rich in history, and offers a breathtaking panoramic view of the surrounding areas, including the ocean, the nearby lagoon and salt pond, and the captivating southern landscape. This historic landmark is well maintained and its grounds are well kept. Its friendly Christian congregation welcomes visitors to join them in worship and the church remains one of Antigua's national treasures.

St. Philip's Anglican Church

St. Philip's Anglican Church is situated in the small town of Ffryes, in the Parish of St Philip. The first church of the parish was founded in 1690 and was a wooden structure, located in Willoughby Bay, close to the coast. In 1713, a proposal to build a new and more centrally located parish church was put forward, but received opposition from some parishioners. It is unclear how this controversy was settled, however, in 1830, the present Anglican parish church was built and is considered by many as one of the prettiest of its time. There are numerous tourist attractions in the parish including, Half Moon Bay Beach (Freetown), Stingray City (Seatons Village) and the famous Devil's Bridge National Park (near Willikies Village).

St. Philip's Anglican Church is supported by its parishioners, especially through funds donated by members and friends of the Mill Reef Club, a private club established in Antigua in 1947. Over the years, the Mill Reef Fund has helped the church with much needed assistance such as the replacement of the current church roof, maintenance of the church's cemetery grounds, as well as contributing to any required restoration works. The churchyard of this historic church is best described as peaceful, with stunning views of Willoughby Bay. Its garden is an opportunity to enjoy the peace and tranquillity of its wonderful surroundings. Despite the fact that there is not much to see in the town, a stop at the historical church is highly advisable.

St. Peter's Anglican Church

The Anglican Parish Church of St. Peter's is located in Parham, St. Peter Parish. This magnificent masterpiece is an irregular shaped octagonal church constructed in 1840. There were two earlier churches on the location of the current church. The original church was a wood structure built in 1711 and was destroyed by fire. The second church was built in 1754 and then demolished to accommodate the present church. In 1843, the church suffered considerable damage as a result of the earthquake of that year and was further damaged by the earthquake of 1974.

The current St. Peter's Anglican Church was designed by an English man, Thomas Weekes and the head mason was of African descent. It was built with quarry cut stone and without concrete or steel. St Peter's unique and fascinating rib-like wooden ceiling looks like an upturned ship's hull. This unusual designed church is a fine example of Georgian ecclesiastical architecture, which is rarely seen outside of Europe. Its distinctive shape and structure makes it one of the important historical landmarks on the island of Antigua.

St. John's Cathedral Anglican Church

St. John's Cathedral is an historic church located in the city of St John's, St John Parish. It is the principal church of the Diocese of the North Eastern Church and Aruba in the Province of the West Indies. The imposing edifice with its twin towers was called *Big Church* by the planters and was built to hold a congregation of 2,200 persons. The present cathedral is not the only structure to have been built on the hilltop site. Two previous churches also named St John's were constructed in the years 1683 and about 1720 respectively. The first church was a simple wooden building and was said to be

totally destitute of beauty or comfort. The second church was a much larger structure built of English bricks, adorned with fine monuments and had the tower added in 1789.

The destruction caused by the 1843 earthquake, led to the construction of the third and current St. John's Anglican Church. It was built in 1845, opened for worship in 1847 and consecrated as a cathedral on July 25th, 1848. During the time of its erection, the structure was criticised by some ecclesiastical architects as resembling "a pagan temple with two dumpy pepper pot towers." ("Historical sites," n.d.). This architectural marvel overlooks the city and its south gate, which was originally the main entrance is flanked by the biblical figures of St. John the Divine and St. John the Baptist. The Anglican Cathedral is part of the history of Antigua & Barbuda and is well known among tourists. Its remarkable interior woodwork continues to undergo important restoration work, in an effort to restore it to its former glory.

All Saints Anglican Church

All Saints Anglican Church is located in the village of All Saints, St Peter Parish. The chapel was built five years after emancipation, in 1839. It is unclear how it derived the name *All Saints*. The consensus was based on the construction of the chapel close to the border of three parishes namely, St. John, St. Peter and St. Paul. However, in the book *To Shoot Hard Labour 2*, the narrator Samuel Smith recollected having been told by his former white employer that the name preceded the church and was given to the area by some early settlers who came from All Saints in England.

All Saints Village is the second largest in Antigua and Barbuda and was established after a large number of the formerly enslaved began to leave the estates. They built a collection of houses close to the Anglican chapel, resulting in the emergence of the village. The area was a hive of activities and All Saints Cross Road and attracted people from surrounding villages.

In 1974, a severe earthquake shook the entire island and left the church building completely destroyed. This forced the parishioners of All Saints to hold their services in their parish hall. The damaged church building was deconsecrated (transferred to secular use) in January 1975 and rebuilt in 1981. In addition, the subsequent hurricanes of 1995 and 1999 left the church with more damages, after which, it was redesigned and renovated during a one year period from 2000 to 2001.

Inside St. Peter's Anglican Church, Parham

Moravian

Spring Gardens Moravian Church

The congregation at Spring Gardens was established in 1756. It is located on St John's Street within the parish of St John. Before the first church was built in 1762, preaching to the enslaved Africans was made under a sandbox tree, which still stands today in the churchyard. The enslaved men and women took it upon themselves to build the first Moravian church. After working all day under the exhausting sun, they walked many miles through the hills to St. John's, each carrying a large stone on their heads. The stones were used to construct the Moravian Chapel at Spring Garden, St. John's.

The church was later enlarged in 1771 and by 1781, the congregation at Spring Gardens had risen to 3,000 members and this led to a further enlargement of the church in 1787. In 1830, the church

established a Benevolent Society to assist members in Spring Gardens. After emancipation, a new church building was dedicated by Bishop George Wall Westerby in 1854, while the Female Teacher Training College that he founded moved from Lebanon (Seaview Farm) to Spring Gardens (St. John's) in the same year. The Spring Gardens Teacher Training College closed in 1958, having served the community for 118 years, while the church was replaced by the current church in 1964. In 1995, the manse (minister's house) and the church building were destroyed by Hurricane Luis. After the restoration work was completed, the church was rededicated on May 18, 1997. Spring Gardens celebrated 260 years in 2016 and remains the main Moravian Church in Antigua.

Gracehill Moravian Church

Gracehill Moravian Church was the second Moravian Station to be established in Antigua. The congregation was located in a number of areas in the village of Liberta. This historic village was one of the very first independent free villages founded in Antigua (1835) by newly liberated Africans, with the help of Moravian missionaries. The first church was located at Bailey Hill near Falmouth, where enslaved Africans from various plantations teamed up and brought stones and other building

materials at night to build the chapel in 1773. However, due to an increase in membership and unsanitary conditions in 1781, the congregation was forced to relocate to Edgecome Hill (now called as Old Gracehill) in Liberta, where a temporary structure was erected for members to worship. In 1785, a new church was funded and built by members on the same site.

As membership grew again, the congregation came together to construct a bigger building in 1832. This structure was damaged and rebuilt following the severe hurricane of 1845 and lasted until its demolition in 1961. According to Hewlester Samuels "The birth of the village of Liberta", the 1845 hurricane destroyed several Moravian buildings, including the manse and the Old Gracehill School. The present-day site of Gracehill was acquired in 1960 and the church built in 1964 is an impressive limestone building dedicated by Bishop Gubi. In 2006, a major refurbishment project was carried out on the church and it was rededicated in May of the same year. The Church celebrated its 240th anniversary in 2013 and believes that the strength and wealth of Gracehill Moravian Church is derived from the unity of its people.

Cedar Hall Moravian Church

Cedar Hall congregation is located in the village of Jennings (Parish of St. Mary) and was the last to be established before emancipation. The congregation is also made up of members from three nearby villages, Bolans, Ebenezer and Golden Grove. It is said that the village developed around the Moravian settlement, when the church moved into the area in 1821. Later that year, in November, the foundation stone for the new church and the mission house was laid. On Easter Day, April 7, 1822, the church building was consecrated and dedicated for divine worship. Quite early after the Cedar Hall Moravian Church was established, a Sunday school for enslaved children was kept in the cellar of the church, while an evening school for enslaved adults was held on the estate.

Immediately after emancipation in 1834, the Cedar Hall Church School (aka: Cedar Hall Elementary School) was opened. The school was the only one in the community

that educated children from the Golden Grove area to beyond Bolans. Around 1975, the school was handed over to the government and became known as Jennings Secondary School. In 1846, the Moravians established a boys' training school in Lebanon, which then moved to Cedar Hall about a year later. It was a residential school assigned to tutelage boys for seven years, after which they could be admitted for admission to the Mico Teachers Training College. The students were from several islands and were aged 6 and 8 years old. On April 7, 2022, Cedar Hall Moravian Church commemorated its 200th anniversary.

Lebanon Moravian Church

Lebanon Moravian Church was started as a mission in 1837 and is located in the Village of Seaview Farm, St. George Parish. From its elevated position, visitors and parishioners can get a lovely view of the sea in the north-eastern part of the Island. The village was once known for its traditional handcrafted pottery made by women. This tradition of making coal pots and cooking pots, can be traced back to the early 18th century and has all the hallmarks of the skills enslaved people brought with them from Africa. However, this pottery tradition seems to have disappeared, other than at Elvie's Pottery where traditional hand-made pottery is still active in the village to this day.

In 1843, the Moravian Church in Lebanon was one of the victims of the terrible earthquake that struck Antigua and many other small Caribbean islands. According to Moravian records, it destroyed a variety of stone buildings, with a death toll of about 30 people in Antigua. The Moravian settlement in Lebanon is memorable to most Moravians, as it was where the first Teachers' Training College in Antigua was built in 1840, before it was moved to Spring Gardens in 1854. In 1988, this beautiful and welcoming church celebrated the 150th anniversary of the founding of its congregation. Like most Moravian Churches, Lebanon continues to support its very engaged congregation.

Greenbay Moravian Church

Greenbay Moravian Church was established in 1845. It is located in the village of Greenbay, St. John Parish and was built with a government grant of £110 pounds sterling, which was received in December 1844 to assist with the construction of a chapel-school. Greenbay's congregation emerged immediately after emancipation, when many of the formerly enslaved left the sugar estates to settle in St. John's. The church was fortunate to have had the services of the pioneer preacher, John Andrew Buckley who in 1852, became a teacher and assistant preacher and took up the challenge to raise enough funds to expand both the church and school. He was the first person of African descent to be ordained as a Deacon in the history of the Moravian Church, and his ordination was performed at Spring Gardens in 1856 by Bishop George Westerby.

The present church bell was a Christmas gift to the Greenbay congregation from the readers of the Moravian Mission Magazine (USA) in 1930 and it was blessed on April 19, 1931. Remarkably, the old bell once lowered, had the year 1831 inscribed on it, which marks exactly one hundred years of service. In 1967, the present was rebuilt on the same site using concrete and dedicated by Bishop P.M. Gubi. After serving the Greenbay and surrounding communities for many years, a major renovation work was carried out on the present church, which took over twenty years and was completed in 2021. The church was re-dedicated on Sunday July 4, 2021 by the Rt. Rev. Dr. A. Kingsley O'Reilly Lewis. Greenbay Moravian Church has an active and engaging Sunday school, and carries out outreach programmes within the community.

Gracefield Moravian Church

Gracefield Moravian Church is located in the village of Cedar Grove, St. John Parish. The congregation was founded in 1839 and the first church building, which became the eighth Moravian church to be built in Antigua, was dedicated on August 11th 1839. A month after the dedication, a school was opened. Other buildings that were later erected on the grounds of the church, included the mission house or Manse and the school master's House. The specific method used by the formerly enslaved to build the church is attributed to its longevity, as the building survived several major earthquakes and hurricanes. This historic church is now in disrepair and dilapidated, and is in need of major repair and restoration, so as to preserve its historical importance to the Moravian Church and the twin island nation of Antigua and Barbuda.

In the book *Gracefield a Northern Star*, the author, Reverend Leon H. Matthias, shared many Moravian memories. For example, he recalled how the mission house was destroyed by *Hurricane Dog* in August 1950 and that the old church like its successor was built with the belfry. He also made reference to the fact that "Gracefield was the first congregation in the Eastern West Indies Province to welcome an ordained female as a pastor." Further, in 1997, Gracefield made another first by becoming the first Moravian congregation in Antigua to launch a steel band. It was the female pastor by the name of Reverend Athill that challenged the congregation to build a new church. The present church was dedicated on Sunday, October 18, 1987. The community spirit that existed at Gracefield from its inception has continued to this day.

Gracebay Moravian Church

Gracebay Moravian Church is located on top of a scenic hill in the village of Old Road, St. Mary Parish, overlooking Carlisle Bay on the left and Curtain Bluff hotel and beach on the right. The congregation was founded in 1791 and was called Gracebay Mission Station. This third Moravian station acquired land along the sea-shore in 1796 and built the first Gracebay in 1797. The congregation was later renamed Gracebay Moravian Church. In 1811, the congregation was relocated from its original location near Old Road Town to its present location on Manchioneel Hill. In 1838 a permanent school building was erected, which was built by Joseph Brown, the master carpenter and communicant who was also responsible for the construction of various churches and schools.

After surviving many hurricanes and earthquakes, the Gracebay mission house was destroyed by the hurricane 1845, while the disastrous hurricane of September 1928 completely wrecked the Sanctuary. The latter caused heavy casualties and extensive damage along its path and reportedly killed at least 1,500 people in the Caribbean region. On May 22, 1929, a service of dedication was held by the Gracebay congregation in the newly erected Moravian Church. This new structure was built mainly of stone and reinforced, and was capable of seating three hundred people. The foundation stone of the new building was laid on December 16, 1929 by the Governor of the Leeward Islands, His Excellency Lieutenant-Colonel St. Johnston (Moravian Mission, 1930, vol.28, p.76-77). The church was reputed to be among the finest chapels of its kind in Antigua. Another hurricane with a devastating effect was Hugo, whose hurricane-force winds in 1989 removed the roof of the school house. Before this event, the Moravian school house in Gracebay was the only one of its type that was still standing. The view from Gracebay is truly stunning and something worth seeing.

Cana Moravian Church

The Congregation at Cana was founded between 1881 and 1883, and is situated in the village of Swetes, St. Paul Parish. The village bears the name of the plantation owners during the 1700s. The development of the village started in the mid-1840s, when the owner of the plantation at the time set aside part a portion of land for sale to the formerly enslaved. Despite the long existence of its congregation, the church had no permanent location until 1950. The site where the church was built was given to the Swetes congregation by the government of Antigua and Barbuda, in exchange for lands at Old Road (Gracebay).

In April 1957, the foundation laying ceremony was held in Swetes for the commencement of the construction of the new church. On January 25, 1958, the new church was dedicated at Cana in Swetes by Bishop Peter Gubi of St. Kitts. According to *The Wachovia Moravian* (Winston-Salem, N. C., May, 1959), the dedication was a glorious event and the building is considered to be one of the loveliest churches in the Caribbean. The funds needed to construct the church was a joint venture between the Cana congregation and American Moravians, with the American church matching dollar for dollar in a fund raising campaign. In addition, the drawing of the church plan and the supervisory work were done by Mr. S. Benjamin, a member of the congregation who generously donated his time. In 1989, a Moravian pre-school was established in the village of Swetes.

Methodist

Ebenezer Methodist Church

The Ebenezer Methodist Chapel is located on St. Mary's Street in St. John's. It was built on land granted by the legislature (the Government) and dedicated on February 10, 1839. However, this historic edifice is not the first Methodist church in St. John's. The first Methodist chapel, which is generally known as the *First Ebenezer*, was erected on Tanner Street, St John's in 1783. The chapel was a wooden structure with a capacity of 2000 persons. It was recorded as the first Methodist chapel to be built in the Caribbean and served the congregation until the construction of the present building or second Ebenezer, which was built to accommodate the growing membership. However, over the years, the chapel has undergone several major renovations and restorations, due to natural disasters like the earthquakes of 1843 and 1974, and general wear and tear.

This noble building is regarded as the mother church of Methodism in the Caribbean, and it remains a landmark in the history of the Methodist Society in Antigua. In 2019, Ebenezer Methodist Church held an Anniversary Awards Banquet to celebrate 180 years at the present location under the theme "Through God's Grace and Mercy, We Celebrate 180." The congregation at Ebenezer run three significant outreach programmes, including an after school programme that supports students with their homework, meals on wheels service for the less able, and a health clinic.

Parham Methodist Church

Parham is a small quite coastal town and port, which is located in the north-east of Antigua. It is one of Antigua and Barbuda's oldest trading towns and had a sugar plantation operating in 1679. Early records of Parham situated in the Parish of St. Peter show that Methodist work existed in the town as early as 1763. This was according to Francis Gilbert, brother of Nathaniel Gilbert, founder of Methodism in Antigua, who made reference to preaching at Parham as part of his one-year crusade (1763-1764). Although, there is no official date of when the first Methodist chapel was built in Parham, it is understood that this chapel was destroyed along with all church records in 1802.

The present church was built in 1809 and consisted of a mission house and an adjacent school room. Over the years, the church membership increased and the Methodist community grew. However, due to a continued deterioration of the church buildings, the Synod in 1962, decided to renovate. This included adding a manse on top of the church hall to accommodate an additional minister. Parham Methodist Church is an historic church that has continued to give dedicated service to members of its congregation.

Gilbert Memorial Methodist Church

Gilbert Memorial Methodist Church is located at Zion Hill in the Parish of St. Philip and was named in honour of Nathaniel Gilbert, the founder of Methodism in Antigua. Historical records indicated that Zion Hill was a thriving community and may have been the place where the enslaved from Gilbert's estate erected their first chapel, due to its close proximity to the estate. Evidence of Methodist work in this area seems to have started in the early 1800's. This was confirmed in David Farquhar's Caribbean Adventures, where he presented entries from Reverend Thomas Hyde's journal for December 1821 and March 1822, preaching in a chapel at Zion Hill.

Another story of a second Wesleyan Church on Zion Hill was said to have been built after 1821 and before 1834, by Mr. and Mrs. Taylor for the enslaved on their estate and those nearby. Interestingly, the present chapel has the year 1843 written on its front, but the year appears to be more associated with when it received government grant to enlarge or renovate the structure. On the whole, it is most likely that the present chapel is the same as the one built by the Taylors. Some have called Gilbert Memorial 'the Methodist shrine of the Caribbean', due to the chapel housing three stones which testify to its historical importance and antiquity. In fact, two of the stones came from the steps of his house where Gilbert preached to the enslaved. Gilbert's house is now the Ecumenical Agricultural Centre in Mercer's Creek. Although, this historic church has been renovated and upgraded over the years, it still retains most of the trinitarian architectural qualities of the older building.

Bethesda Methodist Church

The history of Methodism in the village of Bethesda, St. Paul Parish dates back to the early 1800s. Methodists constructed the first classroom for enslaved children in the Caribbean at the area that would later become known as Bethesda Village. Enslaved Africans from Blake's estate and other adjacent estates built the structure. Vigo Blake, the slave headman, conceived of the school, which opened on May 29, 1813. At this time, the Methodists met and worshiped in a building at Willoughby Bay. The building, along with others, was destroyed in the 1843 earthquake. Consequently, most of the population of Willoughby Bay moved to Freetown, where a Methodist chapel was built to accommodate them. However, a meeting place was established near Blake's Estate. The old schoolroom was demolished because it was dilapidated, and a chapel named after the original school was built on the site. Overcrowding forced the expansion of the chapel in 1847.

In 1871, a new wooden chapel with enough space for the school was built to serve as a place of worship for the Christian Hill and Bethesda Methodist congregations. After that, significant repairs were made in 1912. Following the two successive hurricanes of 1950 (August 21 & 31), the chapel served as a refuge for many residents of Bethesda village. As a result of a church conference in 1970, approval was granted for a new chapel. This started with the construction of a church hall that served as a place of worship until the new concrete chapel was finished and dedicated in 1975. On September 5, 1995, Hurricane Luis made landfall and wrecked a number of structures, including the roof of the church. Bethesda Methodist Church celebrated its 150th anniversary of continued worship on December 5, 2021.

Baxter Memorial Methodist Church

Baxter Memorial Methodist Church is the name of the Methodist Church at English Harbour (Parish of St Paul). It is located in the southern part of the island and is 16 miles from the capital city of St John's. The chapel serves English Harbour and the villages of Falmouth, Cobbs Cross and Piccadilly. The church was named after John Baxter, a white shipwright from England, who arrived in Antigua on April 2, 1778 to work in Nelson's Dockyard. While working on ships, Baxter started to preach part time to the enslaved in a small house called *Baxter's House* in Nelson's Dockyard. When the house became too small, he began to meet at the home of Methodist benevolent, Charles and Elizabeth Thwaites. It was through the efforts of Elizabeth Thwaites and her sister Ann Gilbert, both born into one of the very few slaveholding Black families, that the first Sunday school in the West Indies was opened at English Harbour on 29th May, 1809.

According to Methodist records, there was a wooden structure built in 1846 for the followers of Methodism in the area. This was destroyed by the hurricane of 1848. It is also known that a two-storey wooden structure existed and was destroyed by the 1924 hurricane. Three years later, in 1927, a new chapel constructed with concrete was dedicated. In 1962, the chapel was extended to include a vestry. During the celebration of the 50th anniversary celebration of the 1927 chapel held in 1977, the congregation was renamed *Baxter Memorial* in memory of John Baxter. Furthermore, the hinges of the shutters of the old chapel were donated to Gilbert Memorial for its renovation project. The present Baxter Memorial Church was dedicated in February 1999, while the 1927 chapel was demolished in 2007.

Freemansville Methodist Church

The first Methodist church at Freemansville (aka: Freeman's Village), St. Peter Parish, was established around 1872. It was about 1.5 miles north-west of the present church in the old village. After the abolition of slavery in 1834, Freemansville, then called Franchibelle or Francibell, became the second free village to be established in Antigua. In 1852, the village was featured in what is now a vintage map. The emergence of Methodism at Freemansville was allegedly brought by enslaved women from

the nearby North Sound Estate. As stated in the book, *To Shoot Hard Labour*, in 1890, Freemansville consisted of a Methodist church and twelve houses.

For many years, Methodist influence dominated Freemansville and surrounding estates such as Freeman's, Belle View, Sanderson's and Jonas. According to Methodist history, the site of the first church was affected by the heat of the sun and the flint stones that caused grass fires. To correct this problem, the second chapel built in 1910 was constructed on higher ground. The church building was used as a shelter for the local community during the hurricanes of 1923 and 1950. However, the second chapel was seriously damaged by a number of hurricanes as well as termites, leading to the construction of a third building with reinforced concrete and concrete blocks. As the congregation grew, it became necessary to construct a new and larger chapel. The building of the fourth chapel, which began in 1999, was halted and restarted again in 2009, for a number of reasons. The new chapel is currently under construction and shows every sign of being a magnificent structure when completed.

Gilbert Memorial Methodist Church

Roman Catholic

St Joseph's and St Patrick's Catholic Church

St Joseph's and St Patrick's Catholic Church was completed in 1909. It was constructed on the site (corner of Independence Avenue and Church Street) of the first Roman Catholic Church, which was erected in 1869. The original church was replaced due to the growth of the Catholic population. This new and bigger church became a pro-Cathedral when the Diocese of St. John's-Basseterre was created in 1971.

The earthquake that shook Antigua, and the neighbouring islands on October 8, 1974 was devastating and measured 7.5 on the Richter scale. It damaged the church and various other buildings on the island. The total property damage to Antigua at the time was around EC $60million. In 1981, the church decided to construct a new cathedral. This was achieved in 1987, with the construction of the Holy Family Cathedral. The historic St Joseph's and St Patrick's Catholic Church is in need of reconstruction and renovation, and the Catholic Church has made a commitment to that effect. Once it is renovated, it is expected to be used as a museum and information centre.

Our Lady of Perpetual Help Church

Our Lady of Perpetual Help (OLPH) is a Roman Catholic Church built and opened for divine worship in 1932. Before becoming Tyrells Parish Church in 1958, OLPH was considered an outstation of St Joseph's and St Patrick's Catholic Church in St. John's. OLPH church is located on Roman Hill, Tyrells village (St Paul Parish) near Liberta. It was built to meet the needs of the Catholics in communities like All Saints, Swetes, Liberta, Buckley's, John Hughes and Falmouth. There are two stations attached to OLPH Parish, namely The Good Shepherd Church in Sea View Farm (St. George Parish) and Our Lady of Mount Carmel in Willikies Village (St. Philip Parish). Over the years, other Catholics churches/chapels have emerged in places such as Ovals, Potters, Villa and Parham.

The OLPH church is popularly known as the pink church on the hill, due to its striking pink colour, size and architecture. The church is situated within the Roman Catholic Diocese of St. John's - Basseterre. The diocese covers five Eastern Caribbean islands, including Antigua and Barbuda, St. Kitts and Nevis, Anguilla, Montserrat and the British Virgin Islands. As part of its main fundraising activity, OLPH organises an annual Harvest Bazaar for Parish Development. The lovely OLPH is a photogenic and beautiful historic landmark and welcomes all visitors on their way to English Harbour.

Conclusion

All the historical churches mentioned in this book are part of the history of Antigua & Barbuda. Most have existed for centuries and range from large magnificent masterpieces to those that could only accommodate a small number of worshippers. In those early years, these churches became the centre of community life, as a number of villages sprang up around them. Prior to the government taking control of running the school system, the churches had full responsibility for the education of congregations and the surrounding communities. Besides, the churches also served as schools or educational centres, before the construction of permanent school houses. Although some of these historical churches have been maintained to some extent, there are others that are currently in poor condition and require extensive repair and restoration. While many of these churches have experienced devastating hurricanes and horrible earthquakes, some have been identified as hurricane shelters.

There is no doubt that several of these churches had congregations before they were built. Even while enslaved, these tireless people set aside time and laboured to build these churches. The formerly enslaved did not hesitate to contribute to the maintenance, renovation, and construction of church buildings from the meagre pay they started getting when slavery was abolished. Despite the decline in membership across all denominations, it is clear that many historical churches have stood the test of time and continue to play an important role in the lives of their followers and local communities. They continue to offer spiritual and emotional support, tangible services, and social assistance to members of the congregation.

> *"Until the lion learns how to write, every story will glorify the hunter"* - **An African Proverb by Chinua Achebe (Author of the novel: Things Fall Apart).**

References:

1. Adiele, P. O. (2017). *The Popes, the Catholic Church and the Transatlantic Enslavement of Black Africans 1418-1839*. Hildesheim: Georg Olms Verlag.
2. Anonymous. (1844) *Antigua and the Antiguans: A Full Account of the Colony and its Inhabitants*, Vol. 1. London: Saunders and Otley.
3. "Church apologises for slave trade" (2006). *BBC News*. 8 February. Retrieved from: http://news.bbc.co.uk/1/hi/uk/4694896.stm
4. Aymer, P.L. (2016) *Evangelical Awakenings in the Anglophone Caribbean: Studies from Grenada and Barbados*. New York: Palgrave Macmillan.
5. Baker, G.S. (1973). *Three Hundred Years of Witness*. England: Alan Pooley Printing Ltd
6. Catron, J.W. (2008). *Across the great water: Religion and diaspora in the black Atlantic*. PhD dissertation. Gainesville. University of Florida. Retrieved from: http://ufdcimages.uflib.ufl.edu/UF/E0/02/24/85/00001/catron_j.pdf
7. Donington, K. (2014). *The Legacies of British Slave-Ownership*. History Workshop, 3 November. Retrieved from: https://www.historyworkshop.org.uk/the-legacies-of-british-slave-ownership/
8. Doyle, A. (2017). 'The 2nd largest bailout in British history and its economic effects.' *Bond Vigilantes*. September 6. Retrieved from: https://www.bondvigilantes.com/insights/2017/09/2nd-largest-bailout-british-history-economic-effects
9. Dunn, R.S. (1972) *Sugar and Slaves: The Rise of the Planter Class in the English West Indies*, 1624-1713. Chapel Hill: University of North Carolina Press.
10. Findlay, G.G. and Holdsworth, W.W. (1921). *The History of the Wesleyan Methodist Missionary Society*. London: The Epworth Press.
11. Forde, M. and Paton, D. (2012) *Obeah and Other Powers: The Politics of Caribbean Religion and Healing*. Durham & London: Duke University Press.
12. Gerbner, Katharine Reid. (2013). *Christian Slavery: Protestant Missions and Slave Conversion in the Atlantic World, 1660-1760*. PhD dissertation. Boston. Harvard University.
13. Gracehill Moravian Church (2013). *240th Anniversary Commemorative Magazine*. Antigua and Barbuda: Unknown
14. Gumbs, W. (2007). *Methodism in the MCCA-Its past, present and future*. St. Thomas, U.S. Virgin Islands: Supreme Printing
15. HAS (2011). *The Shanty Tribe of Breaknock*, January-March (Ed). Retrieved from: https://www.antiguanice.com/v2/documents/Newsletter%201st%20qtr%202011-pdf%20final.pdf
16. History.com editors. (2018). *Great Awakening*. Retrieved from: https://www.history.com/topics/british-history/great-awakening
17. Historical sites (n.d.). Retrieved from: http://antiguahistory.net/Museum/Historical.htm
18. Hutton, J.E. (1909). *A History of Moravian Missions*. Fetter Lane, London: Moravian Publication Office.
19. Kaye, M. (2005). *1807-2007: Over 200 years of campaigning against slavery*. London, UK: Anti-Slavery International
20. Klein, Herbert S. (1966). Anglicanism, Catholicism, and the Negro Slave. *Comparative Studies in Society and History*, vol.8, no. 3, (1966), pp. 295-327.
21. Kirton-Roberts, Winelle J. (2015). *Created in Their Image: Evangelical Protestantism in Antigua and Barbados, 1834-1914*. Bloomington, Indiana: AuthorHouse.
22. Knight, E. V. (2009) *Growing Up in All Saints Village, Antigua: The 1940s - the Late 1960s*. USA: Xlibris Corporation.
23. Lamport, M.A (ed.) (2018) *Encyclopedia of Christianity in the global south*, vol 2. London: Rowman & Littlefield.
24. Methodist Church Antigua (2010). *Our Methodist Story: 250th Anniversary Commemorative Magazine*. Antigua and Barbuda: Antigua Printing and Publishing Ltd
25. Mhaka, T. (2023). "Apologies for slavery are commendable, but not nearly enough." *Aljazeera.com*. Retrieved from: https://www.aljazeera.com/opinions/2023/1/19/apologies-for-slavery-are-commendable-but-not-enough
26. Milwood, R.A. (2007). *European Christianity and the Atlantic Slave Trade: a Black Hermeneutical Study*. UK: AuthorHouse
27. Morris-Chapman, D.P. (2019*).* 'John Wesley and Methodist responses to slavery in America.' *Holiness: The Journal of Wesley House Cambridge* Vol. 5 (1), pp. 37-58. https://doi.org/10.2478/holiness-2019-0003.
28. Moore, Robert. (2010). *Anglicanism and the Abolition of Slavery*. Retrieved from: https://www.anglican.ca/wp-content/uploads/2010/11/15-moore.pdf
29. Moravian missions (1930). An Illustrated Record of Missionary Work. *News from the mission fields (West Indies: Antigua)*, vol. 28. (No. 10), p.76-77. London: Moravian Mission Agency
30. Neal, J. (2013). *William Warrener's Contribution to Methodist Missionary History*. Retrieved from: http://www.methodistheritage.org.uk/missionary-history-neal-william-warrener-2013.pdf

31. 3. Newcomb, S. (1992) *Five Hundred Years of Injustice: The Legacy of Fifteenth Century Religious Prejudice*. Shaman's Drum. p. 18-20. Retrieved from: http://ili.nativeweb.org/sdrm_art.html
32. Ngonya, K. W. (2009). *Kongolese Peasant Christianity and Its Influence on Resistance in Eighteenth-and Nineteenth-Century South Carolina*. Masters of Arts. Columbus: The Ohio State University.
33. Olusoga, David. (2015). "The history of British slave ownership has been buried: now its scale can be revealed." *The Guardian*. 12 July. Retrieved from: https://www.theguardian.com/world/2015/jul/12/british-history-slavery-buried-scale- revealed
34. Olwig, Karen Fog. (1990). 'Struggle for Respectability: Methodism and Afro-Caribbean Culture on 19th Century Nevis.' *New West Indian Guide* 64 (3&4): 93-114.
35. The Obeah Act, 1904, CO 154/12, The National Archives, UK. Retrieved from: https://obeahhistories.org/1904-leeward-islands-act/
36. Painter, J. (2021). *Anglican Missionaries in the British Caribbean, Before Abolition*. Master of Arts. University of Essex.
37. Painter, K. (2001). .The Pro-Slavery Argument in the Development of the American Methodist Church.' *Constructing the Past*: Vol. 2: Iss. 1, Article 5. Retrieved from: https://digitalcommons.iwu.edu/cgi/viewcontent.cgi?article=1061&context=constructing
38. Render, B. (2017). *The Slaves' Devil: The Parallel between Experiences of Slavery and Christian Conversion*. Masters of Arts. Georgia State University. Georgia.
39. Ross, Emma George. *African Christianity in Kongo*. In Heilbrunn Timeline of Art History. New York: The Metropolitan Museum of Art, 2000. Retrieved from: http://www.metmuseum.org/toah/hd/acko/hd_acko.htm (October 2002)
40. Samuel, Hewlester A. (2007). *The Birth of the Village of Liberta, Antigua*. Coral Springs, Florida: Llumina Press
41. Smith, K. & Smith, C. (1986). *To Shoot Hard Labour: The life and times of Samuel Smith, an Antiguan workingman 1877-1982*. Edan's Publishers. Toronto, Canada.
42. Smith, K. & Smith, C. (2003). *To Shoot Hard Labour 2: The life and times of Samuel Smith, an Antiguan workingman 1877-1982*. Edan's Publishers. Toronto, Canada
43. Taylor, P. and Case, F.I. eds. (2013). *Encyclopedia of Caribbean Religions*, Volume 1 A- L; Volume 2: M-Z. Champaign, Illinois: University of Illinois Press.
44. The Diocese of St. John's-Basseterre (2021). *50th Anniversary 1971-2021*. Antigua and Barbuda: Unknown.
45. Moravian Church (2006). *250 years establishing, educating, empowering people for God*. Antigua and Barbuda: Sun printing & publishing (Antigua) Ltd.
46. Thomas, H. (1997). *The Slave Trade: History of the Atlantic Slave Trade, 1440-1870*. London: Picador
47. 47 Thome, J. A. and Kimball, J.H. (1838). *Emancipation in the West Indies. A six months' tour in Antigua, Barbados, and Jamaica, in the year 1837*. New York: The American Anti- Slavery Society.
48. Voncujovi, S. (2020) *How African Spirituality Got Tied to Satan*, Sena Voncujovi, 30th June. Retrieved from: https://humanparts.medium.com/why-african-spirituality-became- associated-with-satan-a16712cf9cdf
49. Walvin, J. (2008) Slavery, the Slave Trade and the Churches. *Quaker Studies*: Vol. 12: Issue. 2, Article 3. Retrieved from: https://digitalcommons.georgefox.edu/quakerstudies/vol12/iss2/3
50. Williams, Eric. (1944). *Capitalism and Slavery*. Chapel Hill: University of North Carolina Press.
51. Woodson, Carter G. (1977). *The Mis-Education of the Negro*. New York: AMS Press. (First published 1933).
52. Wyatt, T. (2020). "Clergy gained compensation equivalent to £46 million today, at abolition of slavery." *Church Times*. Retrieved from: https://www.churchtimes.co.uk/articles/2020/26-june/news/uk/clergy-gained- compensation-equivalent-to-46-million-today-at-abolition-of-slavery
53. Zacek, N. (2013). West Indian Echoes: Dodington House, the Codrington Family, and Caribbean Heritage. In M. D., & A. H. (Eds.), *Slavery and the British Country House* (1st ed., pp. n/a-n/a). English Heritage.
54. Zacek, N. (2017). The Caribbean and West Indies. In J. Gregory (Ed.). *The Oxford History of Anglicanism: Establishment and Empire, 1662-1829* (1st ed., vol. II, pp. 189). University of Oxford.
55. Zehavi, Ben. (2019). "19th Century Slave Bible that Removed Exodus to Repress Hope Goes on Display." *Times of Israel*. March 29. Retrieved from: https://www.timesofisrael.com/19th-cent-slave-bible-that-removed-exodus-story-to- repress-hope-goes-on-display

Opposite: Top Row L-R: Bethany Moravian Church, Pigotts Village; Bolans Methodist Church, Bolans Village & Freetown Methodist Church, Freetown Village. Middle Row L-R: Five Islands Moravian Church, Five Islands Village; Newfield (Enon) Moravian Church, Newfield Village & Potters Moravian Church, Potters Village. Bottom Row L-R: Sawcolts Methodist Church, Sawcolts Village; St. Luke's Anglican Church, Bendals Village & St. Stephens Anglican Church, Seatons Village.

Other Historical Churches.